Cotsv
A to Zed

*The Adventures & Reflections
of a Retired Woman in the UK*

MARILYN HONEA

Powerful You!
PUBLISHING
Sharing Wisdom ~ Shining Light

Cotswold Musings: A to Zed
The Adventures & Reflections of a Retired Woman in the UK

Copyright © 2021

All rights reserved. No part of this book may be reproduced by any method for public or private use–other than for "fair use" as brief quotations embodied in articles and reviews–without prior written permission of the publisher.

The intent of the author is to provide general information to individuals who are taking positive steps in their lives for personal, emotional and spiritual well-being. If you use any of the information in this book for yourself, the author and the publisher assume no responsibility for your actions. Readers are encouraged to seek the counsel of competent professionals with regards to such matters.

Powerful You! Publishing is committed to publishing works of quality and integrity. In that spirit, we are proud to offer this book to our readers; however, the story, the experiences, and the words are the author's alone.

Published by: Powerful You! Inc. USA
powerfulyoupublishing.com

Library of Congress Control Number: 2021909341
Marilyn Honea—First Edition

ISBN: 978-1-7356579-2-9

First Edition May 2021

HUMOR / Cultural, Ethnic & Regional

DEDICATION

To Barry, my friend and guide through the Cotswolds. Thank you for introducing me to the most beautiful area in the United Kingdom.

To my family, with gratitude for the years of love and support of my summer sojourns.

To my sister-friend Delia, for welcoming me into your family.

Table of Contents

Introduction — vii
Author's Note — vix

Chapter 1 ~ Life and Death Decisions — 1
Chapter 2 ~ Planning: Nuts and Bolts — 5
Chapter 3 ~ Living Outside of the USA — 11
Chapter 4 ~ Preparing for the Journey — 13
Chapter 5 ~ Living With My Decisions — 17

Musings: A to Zed

A ~ Addressing the Locals — 23
B ~ Bacon, Bar-B-Que, and Burgers — 31
C ~ Communion and Community — 39
D ~ Duvets and Distractions — 45
E ~ Elders and Escalators — 51
F ~ Forks, Fish, and Fickle Friends — 59
G ~ Glorious Gardens and Guilty Pleasures — 65
H ~ Hymns to Hedgehogs — 71
I ~ Idyllic Iona — 75
J ~ Jackdaws — 81
K ~ Kitchen Electrics — 85
L ~ Lords/Ladies and Liquids — 87
M ~ Methodists and Music — 93
N ~ Naughty and Nice — 99
O ~ Olimpicks, Olympics, and Other Oddities — 103
P ~ People of Purpose & Postal Perks — 109
Q ~ Queue Quietly — 125
R ~ Raindrops on Rooftops — 131

S ~ Sights, Sounds, and Scones	137
T ~ Travel, Tea, and Tubs	145
U ~ Unexpected	161
V ~ Visions	169
W ~ Wandering, Waiting, and Wellies	173
X ~ X-Rays	181
Y ~ The Year 2020	185
Z ~ Zenith	189
About the Author	192
Acknowledgments	193

INTRODUCTION

This book is separated into two parts. The first chapter tells my story as a retired widow in search of an adventure. Until that point, I had lived a life punctuated by planned goals, predictable events, and always with an eye to the future. What I aspired to now was a life in the present, filled with serendipitous moments that redefined my outlook as well as expanded my everyday perspective. Who am I? I am anyone I want to be, within my current intellectual and financial constraints.

I chose to discover this new perspective in England, far outside my comfort zone of Southern California. I know I could have chosen a part of the world more divergent from my current culture or climate, but remember my age—there was only so much new information this "senior citizen" desired to absorb.

Chapters 2 to 5 encompass some "dos and don'ts" for those who decide to embark on an adventure outside the USA. If that is not something you are interested in, feel free to go directly to the "musings" section and enjoy my mistakes and perspectives of a new and different culture. Most of my encounters were amusing but the telling of them is in no way intended to make fun of the British culture or people. It is simply my attempt at lighthearted entertainment and an indication of how one's lifestyle can change when embracing a serendipitous outlook.

I hope you enjoy reading these musings as much as I have delighted in compiling them over the past eight years. Names of the citizens in my "little village" have been changed to protect their privacy and in hopes of maintaining the friendship of these adorable people.

The summer of 2020 would have been my ninth in the UK, but my plans, like those of so many others, were postponed until the following year due to the worldwide pandemic. Instead of pining away for my little village (though I did indulge in this a bit), I decided to use the time of isolation to compile my experiences for the delight of others. By the time you read this, I will be back in the UK and living the good life I love so dearly. I hope you enjoy the read and expand your horizons to include new adventures and perspectives.

Marilyn Honea, 2021

"Travel far enough, you meet yourself." ~ David Mitchell, Cloud Atlas

AUTHOR'S NOTE

When one retires, interesting things begin to change. Body parts droop, eyesight blurs, hearing diminishes, and smells become less tolerable. But the mind—that is a different kettle of fish. It begins to question everything of your existence. Have you fulfilled your expectations and goals? Have you been a contributing member of society? Will you leave the world a better place? And the biggest question of all: What the heck are you going to do now?

If I were a good Brie cheese or Merlot wine, aging would be a process of improvement, of reaching my full potential. But what are the expectations of aging in humans? Is this the time when we slow down, think less, and stop dreaming? That is the juncture I faced after turning sixty-two. All of my life I had identified myself as my parents' daughter, my husband's wife, my children's mother, my church's volunteer, my school district's employee, my friend's confidante, and my neighbor's keeper. Now, for the first time, I was asking "Who am I, really?" The answer appeared to be somewhere between "What have I missed?" and "What do I want to become?"

Do you remember your high school yearbook, how under each senior's picture was a list of their accomplishments over the past four years? We judged ourselves, and each other, by the number of those accomplishments, and the one with the longest list won! That was easy compared to what I faced now: a crossroads of redefining myself and clarifying my dreams in my golden years. In the past, I didn't feel as though I existed without the camaraderie of others. Could I function as a single entity? Did I have what it took to face the future with a plan of my own? Could I carry it out solely for the purpose of my own pleasure? So many questions to answer.

Stay with me as I fast-forward to the age of seventy-plus, which is more about answers than questions, more about doing than dreaming, and more about enjoying simple pleasures than chasing accomplishments. For me that means leaving my family home for four to six months each year to live in the United Kingdom, six thousand miles away. Now that takes some mettle, and it makes my heart sing so profoundly that I feel compelled to write about it. Single women of the world rejoice; we have some "balls" after all!

I write this book of musings for all the dreamers out there who are afraid to take that first step in making their dreams a reality. Your retirement years can truly be "golden"—a leg of your journey not merely to be endured, but savored. A time in which you can not only maintain (or claim) your independence, but redefine your existence to fit your desires. You may even be an inspiration to someone else, so get up off the couch and start enjoying every moment. It's not too late!

> "...Arise, my darling, my beautiful one, come with me. See! The winter is past, the rains are over and gone. Flowers appear on the earth; the season of singing has come, and the cooing of doves is heard again in our land" ~ Solomon's Song of Songs 2: 10-12

Chapter 1
Life and Death Decisions

My husband and I had a lovely family planned—one boy, one girl. My only hope was that the boy would come first. I was the oldest child in my family and it was difficult setting the standards as a girl. There were just so many restrictions that don't seem to apply to one's male siblings. But alas, our daughter came first, and from the moment of her birth we forgot all about gender privilege and delighted in the arrival of a healthy and beautiful child. Years later, history would repeat itself, in that she gave the same arguments I had used when facing certain barriers as a teenager. Males do get preferential treatment—more lenient rules regarding driving and dating, better jobs, higher pay, and the ability to urinate in a can or behind a tree when traveling. Indeed, we did have a son two years later, which set the stage for this age-old dynamic and added a new twist in our daughter's knickers.

When the children were ready for preschool, I decided to go back to school. I'm not sure what prompted the decision. Was it that dinner out when I ordered a "scotch and wah-wah"? Or was it being relegated at my husband's staff parties to the "spouse table," where the discussion centered around bedwetting and childhood immunizations? Whatever the reason, I was ready to "find myself" out in the big, bad world. Fitting college into our lives and finances was no easy matter, especially on my husband's teacher salary, but with master budgeting and his help with the kids, not to mention his endless emotional support, I completed my BA and Special Rehabilitative Credential in Communicative Disorders. The local school district hired me as a Speech/Language Specialist, working with infants, toddlers, preschoolers, and their parents, which I did while pursuing my master's degree in the evenings. I loved my workplace, I loved my profession, and I loved the students and my fellow staff members. But, alas, the local school district has a way of burning out the most competent educators over time and taking some of the joy out of our profession. That, along with my husband's declining health, led to my decision to retire after twenty-two years.

As a family, we had met our goals of traveling, educating the children and seeing them make their own way in the world, paying off our mortgage and cars, and avoiding service charges on our monthly credit card bills. Except for hubby's health, all was "coming up roses." The only dream we were unable to fulfill was to live overseas for a prolonged period of time. Doctor visits, hospital stays, and eventually hospice services took precedence, and time seemed to stand still for a few years.

There was a fourteen-year age gap between my husband and myself, so we had always been careful about planning for the future, both financially and emotionally. With his help, I also educated myself about our investments and insurance policies so that in the likely event that he died first I would be able to handle things. But nothing quite prepares you for making decisions alone, waking up to an empty house, or slowly erasing bits and pieces of your companion from your home and memories. It's enough to set even the most independent woman adrift in murky waters, and that's where I found myself in 2008 after losing my husband to congestive heart failure. Life became very lonely overnight. Family and friends were very attentive and supportive, but what repairs the hole left in your heart? How does one pick up the pieces and find a new direction while walking alone? I turned to grief books, support groups, counseling, and journaling—all the suggestions from the imaginary book of *Widowhood for Dummies*. All avenues helped over time, but my day-to-day existence was still lonely and unbalanced.

Gradually, I began to take stock of my current life and the direction in which I wanted it to go. After suffering with bad knees for several years, I finally scheduled bilateral knee replacements. I also started assessing and consulting with children suffering from speech and language delays, extremely rewarding work that I would continue to do for the next two years. Being on my own was getting easier, yet there was still something missing from my life.

One day, while enjoying a cup of tea and perusing a lovely magazine of the English countryside, I was reminded of a conversation with my husband. He had laughingly apologized for the small insurance policy he was leaving, but assured me it was adequate for purchasing a security system for our home and a trip to England. My retort, in jest, was, "How thoughtful, but how am I supposed to get back home again?" His comment was, "You probably won't want to come back." He knew me so well. And so the plans began for me to finally take my extended visit to the Motherland. I concentrated my search on the Cotswold region, that range of rolling hills and farmland in the west-central part of England. Far from the fast pace of London, it is known for its natural beauty and has served as inspiration for many artists and writers. Inspiration—that was just what I needed!

In 2012, almost four years after the death of my husband, I took my first solo flight to London, then a train ride to a small village of the Cotswolds. I loved every minute of my six-month stay there, so much so that I would return to the UK for the next seven summers.

Chapter 2
Planning: Nuts and Bolts

The best part of traveling is the planning. I was laid up for over six months recuperating from each of my knee surgeries and had lots of time on my hands to "log in" and dream. Whatever did we do before the Digital Age? Oh yes, I remember, we read books. (How many Fodor travel books do you have on the shelf?)

Though my life in California was quite comfortable, I was yearning for something different. Southern California in particular is nice and warm (sometimes too warm) and has a desert-like terrain; I found I really missed the rain and the lush green countryside that prevails in a more humid climate. Also, my two-thousand-square-foot house is too big for one person, so I was curious to see if I could adjust to smaller quarters for a long-term period. Finally, I was a bit tired of my rural surroundings and wanted to be closer to neighbors and amenities and lovely country walks. These parameters helped drive me in my search of the perfect village in the UK.

I started by looking at the various villages within the Cotswold area. My primary destination was Stow on the Wold. Firstly, I just loved the name. Secondly, I had visited Stow on a previous occasion and loved the nearby villages of Bourton on the Water and Upper and Lower Slaughter. (Don't the English village names just slide off one's tongue like double cream?)

The second consideration was a long-term let of a furnished abode. Initially, I was looking for a lovely thatched cottage with two bedrooms in the center of town. I quickly discovered, however, that renting in Cotswold villages was not a novel idea, but rather a hot commodity costing an arm and a leg. Most were over £350 (roughly $450) per week, and for a six-month stay, that adds up to more than a "holiday." As it turned out long-term, furnished rentals were scarce as well. Again, the Internet contains a wealth of information, but accessing information useful to you requires a bit of patience. In my case, engaging a property manager or real estate agent was the way to go.

In the end, I expanded my search beyond Stow on the Wold and located a house with two bedrooms in a nearby town. From this point forward the town I chose will lovingly be referred to as "my English village," "my little hometown," or "the perfect Cotswold village." I would not wish to influence your search for your perfect place, nor do I want you crowding into mine. I also want to protect the identity of the residents I know and love, so if my secrecy seems a bit selfish, well, I can live with that.

The primary concern with rentals in the UK is payment. Most realty agents do not pay credit card fees. They are not used to renting from people out of the country and prefer payment in Pound Sterling versus US Dollars. I was finally able to talk the agent into a Pay Pal account, but I paid all the fees. We have become too spoiled in the US by flashing our credit cards for any and all expenses and not paying the merchant fees. This was going to be a learning experience at every turn. And yet, I persevered.

There are some necessary essentials to look for in a dwelling when considering a long-term stay. If you are taking your iPad or laptop, Wi-Fi availability is an essential resource for booking events and keeping in touch with those at home.

Microwaves are necessary, but a stovetop and oven are also desirable for a stay of several months. Eating out is lovely for about a week. After that, one will tire of the limited selection, expense, and local culinary delights. Although cooking has never been enjoyable to me, there are only so many frozen dinners one can tolerate. I have never been a fan of lamb, so chicken breasts became a staple for me. And while the British love their vegetables, they rarely serve them *al dente.* You really don't know how limited your palate is until ingesting in another country!

A decent refrigerator is a must, with freezer large enough to make the ice cubes we Americans are so fond of. Typically, British fridges fit under the counter and the freezer is the size of the American car's glovebox! When it comes to getting a decent night's rest, a bed is far preferable to a pullout couch. Do not assume that "extras," such as linens and kitchenware, are provided in a furnished dwelling unless it is listed as a "holiday let." One must also consider whether a long-term rental has a washer or is within walking distance of a launderette. A cleaning service is always nice to have, but not essential. I have found most daily responsibilities in a small cottage or flat can be accomplished within a ten-minute tidy-up.

Transportation was the next concern. I read up on villages within that area, concentrating on local transportation, including buses, trains, and hire cars. I knew I would not be driving in England—just too many roundabouts, sheep crossings, single-lane bridges, and narrow roads. And then there is that habit among the English of placing the steering wheel on the wrong side of the car.

A proper investigation of prospective locations will also include local bus routes, the nearest train station, taxi services, and proximity to surrounding villages. Although one looks forward to walking to local conveniences, a quart of milk and bottle of wine becomes very heavy on the stroll back to your residence. Most village shopping is done daily or biweekly. In determining your degree of mobility, you must consider the weight of one or two carrier bags in addition to your own girth. Over time, I learned to have the bulk of my groceries delivered from a major grocery chain and use the village co-op for small items.

If you are not a walker, you will be limited to the High Street in the Cotswolds. God made this lovely area just so that people could walk them and admire their beauty. The "Cotswold Way" begins in Gloucestershire and follows walking trails for nearly one hundred miles south to Bath. There are people walking at all times of the day and in all types of weather. They are clearly visible by their backpacks and walking sticks. They travel in pairs, sometimes hordes, and are committed to their task. Those of us who are out for an occasional stroll pale in comparison. I am more a window shopper than a hiker, so using the bus to visit other villages was essential for me.

Bus schedules vary per day and route. They do not always stop in the smallest of villages unless you wave them down. If you are dependent on the bus for transportation, be sure it can get you to a substantial village with shops in case your location is lacking in amenities. Do inquire with the driver regarding the availability of day or monthly passes. In England senior citizens ride the bus for free, but one must be a full-time resident to acquire a pass. Bus schedules also vary on weekends, and in the smaller villages buses do not operate on Sunday at all. If you are renting a cottage/house/flat sight unseen, you might want to inquire its location relative to the High Street for shopping and proximity to the bus stop or taxi stand.

Other areas of concern when scouting your location include restaurants, food shops, post office, bank/ATM, library, tourist information center, and proximity to medical care. If this information is not included on the website, email a local real estate agent or inquire with the Chamber of Commerce.

Regarding health services, a senior traveling in the UK may have access to the National Health Service, and they will be treated in the event of an emergency. However, you may be asked to supplement with either insurance or cash if a longer stay in hospital is required. Investigating various overseas insurance policies is prudent and will ease your mind. If you are staying in a village for over a month, it is also advisable to register with the local doctor/surgeon so that someone has access to your medical records. Of course, if you have extensive medical concerns, it may be necessary to have a letter from your physician regarding your past surgeries/treatments and medications. Carry proof of your prescriptions and/or adequate supply for your stay outside of the U.S.

Another consideration is the local weather. The Internet gives you access to weather conditions on a daily and weekly basis. Tracking the weather will give you an idea of how to pack and if you can tolerate the local conditions for a prolonged period of time. For instance, it is not advisable to travel in the UK for longer than six weeks if you do not enjoy the rain. Let's face it, the English countryside is lovely and green for a reason—the water! If you are allergic to rain, one might consider the South of France, Spain, or Italy! Being from Southern California I rarely get the luxury of a rainy season, so this change in climate was one of the things I most desired.

Chapter 3
Living Outside of the USA

If you are considering living outside of the US for an extended period of time, I have some simple suggestions that I learned in my initial investigations on the internet. For example, whether you deal with a private owner or a property agent, it is advisable to agree to and sign a leasing agreement. Whatever understanding you may have thought you had via email or over the phone, there may be hidden costs, so be sure to negotiate a monthly amount that includes all utilities, trash pick-up, Wi-Fi, insurances and local taxes.

Leases may include an inventory of the household goods. Although this is tedious, it may be in your best interest to check it when you first move in or have a walk-through with the owner/agent. Also, documenting any obvious damage to walls, furniture, or appliance operation is advisable, either by informing the agent and noting it in any documentation of date, or taking a picture of the damage with a digital camera that will record the date. There may also be a deposit requested to cover any possible damages that you incur. Be specific as to what the owner/agent may charge you for the deposit, and if possible, have your deposit money returned before leaving town. The further you are away from the property, the more difficult it is to argue your claim. If this is not possible, demand a walk-through before leaving so that you can settle any disagreements before leaving the area.

If you are securing a flat or cottage from overseas, the monetary exchange can be a problem. As I stated before, using your credit card may not always be convenient. You may be able to wire the money, or use a personal check that will cover the exchange rates; however, I find it's best to set up an account with a local bank (inquire beforehand how much cash is required to open the account and be sure to bring at least that much with you). This is what I did shortly after arriving in the Cotswolds for the first time, and it has made things infinitely easier. The account includes both debit and checking services. I keep the account open with a small amount; this way the following year I can simply transfer monies from my home account before heading to the UK.

As you can surmise by now, I pulled off my initial visit with a combination of meticulous planning and a generous amount of faith. I chose to stay six months, which gave me sufficient time to assess the area, set up local banking, and make myself familiar with several local owners and businesses. I also secured my preferred residence for the next visit. What a wonderful feeling it was when I walked back into the same village six to eight months later with my own bank account, library card, and relationships with the local proprietors. My leap of faith, and my investigatory skills had paid off and I love returning to my "happy place" every year.

Chapter 4
Preparing for the Journey

I had traveled to the UK many times in my life, which proved to be a definite advantage when deciding on a long-term stay there. Firstly, I had a certain level of familiarity with, and love of, the country, which was comforting. Secondly, I had the support of my friends at home, most of whom are travelers, and my children, who had also visited the UK and did not have any reservations about my living there for the summers. Knowing my loved ones were cheering me on made the decision so much easier. Now I could move on to the many logistics involved in such an adventure.

Your first area of concern is securing a passport. If you haven't done so, run, do not walk, to the nearest post office and start the ball rolling. Take some time dressing, applying makeup, and practicing your smile in a mirror. Do not treat this assignment lightly! You have no idea how many people will be looking at your image for the next ten years. It should not be an object of amusement shown around the world. No matter how good you look, however, you will come to hate your passport photo well before the expiration date. If you have a current passport, be sure it does not expire within six months of your return home. A new passport can only be applied for from the US, if that is the country of your primary residence.

Spend some time with your local bank. Let them know where you will be and your dates of travel, as well as what bank cards you will be taking with you. Be sure to provide them with your contact number or email so they can alert you of potential fraud, and have their number on hand in case of emergency. Also, familiarize yourself with the bank's website so you can obtain your account information. It behooves you to monitor your account at least weekly for your own peace of mind. I generally take two credit cards from two different banks, just in case one account is compromised, and one debit card as they are much easier to use for small purchases. There may be a transaction fee (around 10%) each time it is used, which is another good reason to open an account at the local bank after you have arrived. Don't even bother with traveler's checks—they are unwieldy, and the bank is never open when you want to cash one. Stores are much more equipped to take credit cards. Notify your credit card holders of when and where you are traveling (outside the USA) and be sure the card does not expire while you are away.

If you have not made your estate plan or will, please take care of this before you leave. Knowing that your affairs are up to date and in order will save you countless hours of sleep in another country. Secure your important papers (will/estate plan, credit card numbers, copy of your passport, etc.) in a safe or safety deposit box that is accessible by a member of your family. Also, make a copy of your durable power of attorney and medical directive to keep with your traveling papers.

You may wish to purchase some medical insurance while overseas. Research the medical status within your country of choice, as well as the insurance you use within the States, for possible complications. There are many insurance alternatives available online, or through travel agents. Also, if you have a significant ongoing medical condition, you may want to secure a letter from your physician regarding your current level of treatment, medications, and concerns. Take along a copy of your prescriptions, as well as a supply that will last for the duration of your stay. It is advisable to establish residency information with a local physician when you arrive at your destination in case an emergency should arise.

I have found it very helpful and recommend you have a list of addresses and phone numbers of relatives, medical and business associates, and friends accessible, either in an address book or on your computer. If you want to keep in contact with others the "old-fashioned way" (i.e. through postcards or letters, rather than email, Skype, or phone), then bringing along pre-printed address labels is a dandy idea. They will save you time in the long run.

You can schedule your trip by booking a flight online, using a travel agent, or calling the airline directly. Over the years, my husband and I had accrued many airline miles with our credit card. Fortunately, we had the benefit of using some of the miles together, but I was always very frugal and insisted on flying coach. After he was gone, you might guess where I placed myself on that plane—you got it, FIRST CLASS! To date, I have had two direct flights from the States to London Heathrow while sipping champagne, eating meals with silver utensils and cloth napkins, and reclining in a bed for a full night's rest. If I can't afford First Class, I choose Business class and my hope is to never enter the "steerage" area again!

(Hint: If you pay your child's college tuition, room and board, and other expenses using a credit card that accrues airline miles, you both win! However, do explain to your child upfront that the education is theirs, and the miles are yours! I remember my daughter assuming those were her miles because we used the credit card for her out-of-state tuition and expenses. Where do the children get these ideas?)

Chapter 5
Living With My Decisions

Although I had done much preliminary investigation as to where I would settle in the UK, nothing quite prepares you for that first moment when you arrive and claim it as your new address. The internet pictures will NOT do justice to the lovely honey-colored buildings, ancient market squares, promontory war monuments, busy local shoppers, and at least one tour bus daily dropping off eager visitors to "your new town." As I mentioned earlier, I quickly acquainted myself with the people working in the shops and tourist information center. Locals use the sidewalk for "meet and greets" with each other and respect the privacy of the occasional visitor; however, I quickly realized that an endearing smile and proper good morning to each I met helped me transition from "visitor" to "resident." In fact, this openness to others was the most beneficial tactic to becoming accepted by the community. Americans have an advantage in this area, as we are generally considered by those overseas as social animals with a happy disposition. This attitude gives us a leg up in getting acquainted and making long-lasting friendships.

I have rented several types of abodes over the years, including a three-story house, a maisonette, a street-level flat, a two-story family house, and a thatched cottage. One summer I moved to two separate villages, spending a month in each. Do I have a preference as to the type of home in which

I stay? Only that it be in "my special village," where I now have acquired the title of "local."

Over the past eight summers there was only one time I returned to California early: when my mother became ill and needed me. Without a second thought I cut my visit short and have never regretted those last few months I got to spend with her. As for my children, I believe they secretly look forward to my lack of interference in their daily decisions for a prolonged period of time. Absence does indeed make the heart grow fonder!

I had always been the researcher and organizer for family trips, so all the "bits and bobs" of preliminary decisions were familiar to me. I had also experienced living alone after my husband died. But as I stepped off the plane in London Heathrow, many doubts circled my head, much like a flock of birds.

Going through Customs can be the initial shocker—forty-five minutes in line just to reach the agent; standing for all this time after losing feeling in your legs during the long flight; and the odor of your fellow travelers in the line after said flight. I have experienced eight different Customs agents over the years, each with their own personalities and concerns. The first year, I was asked to show proof of my financial stability to stay six months. Luckily I had an old ATM receipt in my purse that proved I had money in the bank. The second year, I was asked why I was staying so long, and I responded, "I am researching a book." The next year they asked me to name the friend I was visiting in "my village" and I found I could not readily remember the name of a single inhabitant. Yet another year, when asked the reason for my visit, I told them "I'm writing a book" which by then had become my standard answer. Imagine my surprise when the agent in year seven retorted, "Haven't you finished that book yet?" Who knew that they record your responses? In year eight all the agents were replaced by tiny machines. All I had to do was insert my passport, drop off my claims card, and continue on to collect my baggage—no lines, no muss, no fuss! Don't you just love progress?

As mentioned, I had planned trips before, traveled internationally on several occasions, and lived alone for a couple of years, so many of these preparations were familiar. Were there any surprises? Yes, so many in fact that I began compiling these incidents so I could look back and remember the humor of the many learning experiences. Luckily, humor is my best coping mechanism. I hope you will also be entertained by some of the ups and downs I encountered. Sit back with a "cuppa" and enjoy!

Cotswold Musings: A to Zed

A
Addressing the Locals

Flat Mates

It had been a few years since I lived with anyone, the last person being my husband with whom I shared an abode for forty years. Yes, there are typically adjustments when one has to share; however, with a spouse you are always under the misguided belief that you can train them to be just like you. Ultimately, we are only mildly successful in that department, though of course we never admit to that in public circles.

The first year I arrived in my village, I had the full run of a house—all three floors, two bedrooms, two baths—with no interference from the outside world. After six weeks, I moved to the ground floor studio so that a couple could "let" (rent) the main part of the house. The studio was a newly refurbished flat which consisted of a single room and bathroom. It had a tiny kitchenette, pull-out couch, and small desk for my computer. I secured this "tiny space" in an effort to save money on rent for the remainder of my six-month stay. Somehow, I thought I would have my sweet little maisonette all to myself, with no worries, no disruptions, no stress. (Note to self: In future, there is such a thing as "too little" and a regular bed is never a luxury item.)

I had barely settled into my little downstairs flat when a couple moved in upstairs. This is when I became aware of the lack of insulation between floors in English dwellings. I heard every sound they made as if they were in the room with me, like invited guests. Even though I could not discern individual words, the constant "blah blah blah" was always with me. My upstairs flat mates enjoyed entertaining frequently, though luckily their guests were of retirement age and didn't usually stay out past their bedtime of 9:00 p.m. The downside to this was the relatively high rate of hearing problems among their guests, resulting in a lot of repeated statements or questions and even louder responses. They also tended to be a bit heavy-footed (this may be due to the aforementioned insulation issue), so their every step reverberated through my ceiling with a delightful bass effect.

My flat mates wasted no time in getting comfortable in their surroundings. The gent loved to practice his keyboard, which was slightly out of tune. It appeared he was still learning his craft, as some songs took several days to master. They both enjoyed show tunes, and frequently sang together with the unsteady beat of the keyboard. Most of the songs they chose were just slightly out of their vocal range, and some dissonance was obvious in their duets. They also liked to entertain their guests with their performances, which meant some doubt of the "listening pleasure" for me. Indeed, there were times when I envied their guests' obvious hearing impairments.

My dilemma became how to live out the remaining four months in some sort of harmony (no pun intended). The best solution, I decided, was to make them my "best friends" and elicit the occasional invitation to go upstairs where the footsteps weren't so deafening. But that still left the musical entertainment I must be subjected to during my visit. Of course, I could always join in on the singing and possibly my voice would turn them off the idea altogether. There was also the prospect that they may not want to make my acquaintance, but I rejected that notion outright. After all, I am from Southern California, which makes me just eccentric enough to be an exciting addition to any party.

The thermostat for the radiators was also upstairs. Unknowingly, they left for a weekend and turned down the heat, leaving me to spend the next damp and cold few days rolled up in my duvet! The Cotswold stone walls are beautiful to look at but not at all practical as insulators.

In an effort to save my hearing and my sanity, I changed my routine. For example, I started writing during the day when they were frequently away from home and roaming the city in the evenings when they entertained. The Pub was always open late, but singing patrons there were no better than my flat mates, probably due to the fact that the pub was frequented by the Church's bell ringers, all of them deaf. In the end it would be my iPod and earphones, brought from home, that served as my saving grace.

> "My roommate got a pet elephant. Then it got lost. It's in the apartment somewhere." ~ Steven Wright

Sheep Happens

In the beginning of each June the Cotswold Olimpicks are held on the edge of our village. It's quite a hike up the incline to the mesa where you can enjoy a carnival-like atmosphere, accompanied by musical entertainment and competitive games. These games, which began in 1612 and have remained much the same since, include tugs o' war, foot races, and shin-kicking. At their conclusion a procession of torches, hundreds of them, are carried down the hill into the village. It is a truly beautiful sight.

During this same weekend in 2012, Gary and Clarice, friends from Southern California, happened to be visiting. I was anxious to show them the local sites and charm of the area. We were able to take a bus up the hill to the Olimpick site, but the buses quit running just as we started to leave. Suddenly, we were faced with the daunting prospect of walking the mile downhill. Luckily, a wonderful local couple came to our rescue to guide us into town. This couple were both in their eighties, so we felt if they could do it, we certainly could. The gentleman had lived there most of his life and knew the short cuts through the sheep pastures. Like fools, we trusted him to lead us.

We went downhill through about three different pastures, each separated by a stile surrounded by nettles. Beware of the Stinging Nettles! Each pasture was populated by rams, ewes, and lambs who stared at us as we tramped down their path, trying to avoid twisting our ankles or getting stung by prickers. As we were coming through the last pasture, I felt as if someone was following me. When I turned around, there was a ram's nose about two inches from my hind end. I thought it was so cute and asked my friend to get a picture. The ram had other ideas. One minute I was upright; the next I was looking at the sky with both feet in the air. I had in fact been "rammed" from behind. Well, between the long grass slippery from sheep muck, the steep incline, and my laughter, it took several attempts to get me upright again. All the while, I swear I could hear that ram chuckling and telling the rest of his cohorts about his single-nosed effort in sacking an American tourist. Yes, my friends, "sheep happens" in the villages of England.

The rest of the way home I avoided people as I had a delicate odor emanating from the back of my jeans. Luckily it was dark by the time we reached the village because surely anyone who caught sight of me from behind would have thought I had soiled myself. Still, my story was around the village by the next day (and in fact it would have made it to the US before me had I not sworn my friends to secrecy). True to the English sense of humor, my friends in the wine store asked, "Is the ram all right?"

I wanted to leave my mark on this charming community, but that wasn't what I had in mind!

"Americans used to roar like lions for liberty; now we bleat like sheep for security." ~ Norman Vincent Peale

Archie, the Cat

One morning I was awakened by a freakish sound. At first, I thought it was the neighborhood kitty, but the sound was more like a "yowl" than a "meow." I looked out the front window and across the lane I saw what looked like a large cat strolling up the neighbor's drive. No, not an oversized cat, but a wild cat, like you see in the zoo. I questioned if there was a wild animal park nearby that might have reported an escapee. It was long and sleek, had the markings of a tiger and tufted and pointed ears similar to a lynx. I watched it saunter toward the neighbors' front door. I held my breath that the family would not open the door and find themselves face to face with the creature. Receiving no response at the front door, the cat brazenly leaped the fence into the backyard.

What should I do? I could dash across the lane, quickly introduce myself to the neighbors, and warn them of this most certainly unwelcome visitor. Immobilized by terror that the cat would come to greet me, I dismissed that idea and stayed hidden.

Later that afternoon, I met my neighbor in the village square, quite by accident, and warned her of the morning vision stealthily investigating her property. To my surprise, she laughed and said, "Oh, that was my Bengal cat. His name is Archie."

What a strange name for a cat, I thought. She readily explained why she had given her cat a man's name. When standing outside and calling for the cat to come in for the night, it seemed more appropriate to call out a person's name than the word the British typically use. I could only imagine the spectacle—a classy British lady, standing on her front porch, summoning her "Pussy" to come home!

"In ancient times cats were worshipped as gods; they have not forgotten this." ~ Terry Pratchett

You've Got Mail

There's nothing more exciting when you are away from home than receiving something through the post. You even get excited by the junk mail and embrace the title "occupant" (that's "Ms. Occupant," by the way). One quickly got to know the main attraction in the village, when he knocked on your door to introduce himself as "Postman Pat!" (No, that name's a bit too cliché for my musings; however, he did knock on my door to introduce himself as "Alf" and asked my name for future reference.) Once Alf memorized your moniker, he took on the role of town crier, emergency contact, and purveyor of all good news. One day in August, Alf knocked on the door and commented on all the cards I had received from the USA. "Is it possibly your birthday?" he asked. By the end of the day, everyone I met on the sidewalk wished me Happy Birthday, as Alf had spread "the good news." What a delight!

Alf also checked on the holiday lets, just to make sure all were alive and accounted for—a kind of built-in security device. He was much too dedicated to stop for a cuppa, but would always wave and say, "Good Morning, Marilyn" along the route. To this day, Alf is almost the first person to welcome me after I arrive from Heathrow Airport, and the last person to say goodbye as I leave again for the USA. Even though I have moved several times over the past eight years around the village, Alf still manages to find me and let the locals know that "Marilyn has arrived." What a town treasure! He is one of the people I miss most when I hear my US postman drop my mail in the box without any greeting whatsoever.

As far as convenience goes, the British postman only delivers mail. One does not put out their post, but delivers all mail to the nearest postbox—any one of those shiny, red pillar boxes on the High Street. It's part of one's morning errands in the village and all very civilized.

"I got a postcard from my gynecologist. It said, 'Did you know it's time for your annual check-up?' No, but now my mailman does." ~ Cathy Ladman

B
Bacon, Bar-B-Que, and Burgers

Bacon and Brie on a Brown Baguette

It's lunch time in the Cotswolds, and you can find any number of sandwich items in a pub or restaurant. As I entered the small hotel in my neighboring village, the entryway was embedded with the original cobblestones of the 1800s, which were almost impossible to walk on. I can't imagine how anyone entering the hotel with anything less than sensible shoes could manage to get to the registration desk. The rocks are very large, some five to six inches in length. Although smooth as river rock, they are raised in the middle forming a mound of uneven surfaces on which to tread. Most people walk along the skirting boards (aka baseboards) where the surface is more even. Although the visual effect is beautiful, it is the most impractical entryway I have ever tried to traverse, especially in a hotel.

The hotel pub daily special on that day was brie cheese on a brown baguette with cranberry sauce spread. For no extra cost, you could also get bacon on the sandwich. That, with a glass of wine, was a most delectable culinary event. Although with all the "b" foods, I probably should have had a Bordeaux wine, but my appetite called for a Pinot Grigio, so for consistency's sake we'll just call it a "Binot."

Eating out is very expensive in the UK. However, I do treat myself when I go to another village to either a lovely tea or nice lunch. Quite often anything with bacon catches my eye. British bacon is a luxury item for me. I was raised on what the British refer to as "streaky bacon"—that is, strips of fat with a small amount of meat infused for a striped effect. It cooks up lovely, but shrinks to about half the size from that with which you started. Bacon in the UK comes in slabs of meat with just a small fringe of fat on the outer edge. Because it is pure pork, when cooked it retains its size, about the dimensions of a small adult's palm. What a glorious addition to a sandwich. The result, crunchy bread with a slab of all-meat bacon, brie cheese oozing through the bread, with a touch of cranberry to enhance all the flavors. Now that's a dream sandwich!

There is something quite catchy to eating foods that go together alphabetically. Maybe it just appeals to my sense of order and too many years writing phonological stories for children with articulation problems. However, a practice story comes to mind for the bilabial /b/ about Billy and Betty entering the Bistro for a bite...

"*Life expectancy would grow by leaps and bounds if green vegetables smelled as good as bacon.*" ~ Doug Larson

BBQ—British Style

That first summer, I began accumulating acquaintances by introducing myself to shop agents, greeting passersby on the sidewalk, starting a conversation with fellow bus travelers, and frequenting the tea shoppes. All these efforts helped to break the ice, but nothing compares with being an invited guest to someone's home.

How exciting! I'd received an invitation to a BBQ—British style. First of all, that anyone in their country can plan ahead for a sunny day is quite remarkable. That week, however, had started out gloriously and Barry, the host, was optimistic about the weather. When he called, he expressed his concern that I was only keeping company with the "highbrows" of the village and was making it his personal quest to introduce me to some of "common folk." Well, I knew that was a come-on, as there are no commoners in the whole of the village—they are all unique and quite charming. Still, the invitation was most appreciated, and in hindsight would become even more so, after my quest to find a grilled burger on the Fourth of July. More about that in a bit.

When I arrived, Barry had donned his chef apron and was preparing the grill. This charming ex-fireman, now a tour guide for the Cotswolds, is a man of many talents. Along with his tour business, he is also a public speaker and an incredible artist. His delightful wife assists him in the tour business, as well as keeps a beautiful garden, and reins Barry in whenever needed. Two other couples joined us for dinner. Unfortunately, I have already forgotten their names, but they were equally interesting conversationalists and storytellers. One of the couples was renovating a lovely old cottage, room by room, in their nearby village. That piqued my interest, as it had been a recurring dream of mine since I first traveled to the UK. The gent had also worked on the fire brigade with Barry years ago, so there was no end of their anecdotes.

The other couple had previously owned a garage in the area and knew almost everyone in the village. They also enjoyed motorcycle racing and the wife was an avid sidecar racer, even after several accidents and broken bones. Now, how often do you go to a party and discuss sidecar racing? What a hoot!

The dinner included sausages, ribs, and chicken on the grill. They were all delicious, with accompaniment of potatoes, salad, beans, and a strawberry meringue. The wine flowed freely and the stories got more believable over time. At the end of the evening, I enjoyed my first gin and tonic—such an English thing to drink—which has since then remained a staple among my weekly food groups.

It was about 11:30 when the party broke up. I chose to walk home alone, which appeared safer than have one of them driving me after all that liquor. I'm sure I was a little unsteady on my feet, and probably did not walk a perfect straight line down the sidewalk, but felt wonderfully safe crossing the village at that time of night.

The following day, the weather once again turned to intermittent showers, which I had come to expect daily. The wonderful 'sunny' BBQ is but a memory, but one I will enjoy over and over. It was quite like a BBQ in my own yard in San Diego, with sunshine, good friends, and delicious food. However, rarely do the Southern Californians concern themselves about the weather, as rain there is about as rare as solar lights and sunglasses are in the UK.

"You bring your own weather to a picnic." ~ unknown

In Search of a Burger

It was the Fourth of July and nobody cared—at least not in the UK. That year, I had gotten reports of dry, hot weather across the US, with wildfires out of control in Colorado. My cousin from Indiana said things were so dry they had removed their boat and jet ski from the pond (formerly referred to as a lake), and that there would be no pyrotechnics due to the fire hazard. And yet in the Cotswolds, it continued to rain! I saw the sun about noon and, ever the optimist, immediately hung my wash outside before starting out on a walk. I only got a block before the clouds came back and it started sprinkling on me. I think that was the first time in sixty-five-plus years of life that I had worn a sweatshirt on July 4th! At one point, there were blue skies overhead, and yet it was still drizzling. Will the rain ever stop?

But remaining festive for the holiday, I headed to town in my red, white, and blue outfit in search of anything American. I ordered a bowl of soup at the tea shop which had apples and parsnips (who knows what parsnips are?). The apple soup was the closest thing I could find to an American cuisine. Sad, so sad! What I really wanted was a hamburger.

I stopped in to see several storeowners I knew along High Street, asking where I could possibly order a hamburger. You would have thought I asked for an alien dish. So, I continued on in hopes of meeting someone who might understand the meaning of American Fourth of July. There were no flags except Union Jacks in the Tourist Information Center. No Independence cards in the card shop. I could find ground beef (aka "mince") in the butcher shop, but I would have to bring it home and cook it. That also presented a problem, as I would have to fry it and not have it from the grill. I paused to celebrate with my friends in the La Bel Artist Studio for a while, which felt as American as anything else in the UK. The owners are Hungarian and Indonesian, and my favorite artist from Cambodia was there. Felt just like home!

The next stop was at the public library to ask my favorite librarian friends if they knew where I could get a good burger. They directed me over to the Kings Hotel across the High Street. The hotel had stopped serving for lunch, but would make me a proper hamburger and chips (aka French fries) at the dinner hour starting at 6:30. I am sure they are still talking about the overweight American lady who came in search of a fatty meal, but I couldn't care less. After all, what is July 4th without a hamburger?

I called an acquaintance from church and asked her to meet at the King's Hotel. She eagerly accepted, and we celebrated the Fourth with Angus burgers, which were delicious and almost as good as from the grill at home. Of course, there was no potato salad or baked beans or even a watermelon, but we can't have everything. I had found a little bit of America right here in the village! There were no fireworks, but I was able to get a glimpse of the pyrotechnics from Washington DC on the "telly."

That was my first Independence Day in the Cotswolds. In subsequent years, I made sure there were always a Union Jack and Old Glory flying side by side in my window. I tend to refer to the Fourth of July now as my "Interdependence Day"!

"Guess what the British call Independence Day? 'Thanksgiving.'" ~ source unknown

C
Communion and Community

Communion in the Cotswolds

My little Methodist Church in the UK is absolutely charming. The congregation, all fourteen of them, are each worthy of a chapter in any book. The first year I attended this church I was almost the youngest member. I memorized their names easily, but pronouncing my name presented a bit of challenge to my fellow worshippers. ("Marilyn" in the Kings English is three syllables: /mare a' lin/.)

The members are a thrifty bunch, by US standards. The weekly offering is significantly smaller than my church back home, so even my meager donation is much appreciated. The first Good Friday service I attended the chief congregational concern was whether there would be refreshments after the service. This was not in the weekly budget, but a luxury offered once a month, so everyone was excited to learn that we would indeed be offered hot tea/coffee, accompanied by hot cross buns. (I think we were all looking forward to the food as much as the community with one another).

After the service concluded, five of us sat around a table anticipating the delectable treat. Much to my chagrin, we had one bun to share per table and it was cut into eight pieces. Who knew you could get eight wedges out of one hot cross bun? Makes you wonder if a single pie would serve Parliament? At any rate, we all enjoyed a "taste" of bun and our hot beverage of choice.

Communion is a favorite part of my worship, both at home and traveling. I find it interesting how many different ways churches distribute the "elements," and God and I have had lengthy discussions regarding the symbolism of "His Body" represented by carbohydrates. He knows bread is my weakness and one of those daily food groups in which I tend to overindulge, so why does He tempt me so?

In my California church, we use the intinction method, by dipping a piece of bread torn from a loaf into a chalice of grape juice. We typically have three ten-inch round loaves of bread, broken into six halves. Of course, we serve over two hundred, so we need a significant amount of bread.

That Easter Sunday morning, I headed toward my little village church, where communion was being offered. Yes, we numbered less than twenty, but I was still bowled over to see the bread on the communion table was the size of a dinner roll! Even the pastor was having difficulty stretching the bread to accommodate everyone. The congregants filed up to the communion rail to kneel and receive communion. (The kneeling alone is a deterrent to most seniors.) Breaking up the roll into such tiny pieces also proved difficult. The wine (non-alcoholic in a Methodist Church) was served in those tiny glass cups that fit into the tiny holes on the back of the communion rail. Following service, the cups are washed to be used again next month. I haven't used one of those cups for over fifty years in the US!

I know it is possibly sacrilege to compare communion formats when it is such a spiritually symbolic gesture. But if one has not eaten before church, that large loaf of bread always looks mighty tempting. I must confess, the dinner roll crumbs and grape juice in a thimble did not quench any nutritional cravings; however, the spiritual experience was not lost on the soul. Often it is good to shake up one's mental images so as to challenge the significance of the action.

"It was interesting to think that the very first liquid ever poured on the Moon, and the first food eaten there, were communion elements." ~ Buzz Aldrin

Community

To say that my village is a classless society would be incredibly naïve. Within any given postcode, you can find a plethora of Lords and Ladies—some born into the titles and some who have received them for meritorious efforts. To ignore this posh group of society would be ridiculous of any American. After all, we never get an opportunity to rub elbows with royalty! The trick is to move fluidly between the classes with as little kerfuffle as possible. The Lords and Ladies can open many doors of prominent introductions, particularly for luncheons, afternoon teas, dinner parties, or cocktail gatherings. One very good friend in my village is Lady Jean. Over the years, she has become a mother-away-from-home. I have attended many soirees hosted by Lady Jean and met such wonderful people from various backgrounds. At one point I had the privilege of accompanying her to the House of Lords in London for a Women's Institute Tea. No, I did not get to "take tea with the Queen," but I felt like I had been amongst the upper crust nonetheless. Equally as important were the rainy days Jean and I just sat around the "aga" (aka stove) in her kitchen, talking politics over a cup of tea.

I do remember on one occasion meeting some of the more influential residents over a glass of wine or cup of tea and finding them a bit stuffy, but no more so than acquaintances in the US. On that occasion, as I was introduced, a churlish older woman asked me, "How are things in the Colonies?" Now that made me laugh, but she never cracked a smile. Possibly the English history books have not be updated in a while!

On the other hand, the community as a whole has treated me most graciously and welcomed me into the neighborhood with the upmost respect. They really don't ask me about my social standing in America or act as though it would make any difference in their treatment of me.

I have had tea in the best of china and wine in a tumbler—both equally tasty and enjoyable. We Americans tend to romanticize the English sense of decorum, but they put on their knickers one leg at a time, just as we do.

C - Communion and Community | 43

> DEJA POO: The feeling that you've heard this crap before.

FAVORITE PUB SIGN

"The middle class were invented to give the poor hope; the poor, to make the rich feel special; the rich, to humble the middle class." ~ Mokokoma Mokhonoana

D
Duvets and Distractions

Duvet Stuffing

I was lying on the couch breathing rapidly, my forehead dripping with perspiration, and I was positively knackered! Now I know all kinds of visions are going through your naughty little minds—"Marilyn is really getting up close and personal with some of the neighbor chaps"; or, "Marilyn is really serious about weight loss and has chosen to walk several miles along the Cotswold path"; or, "Marilyn has finally given in to her age and is just winded walking between the rooms of her tiny flat." Well, you are all wrong!

The British have this wonderful device on their beds that will keep you warm in the coldest of weather. They are like a feather mattress that takes all your body heat and surrounds you with delightful warmth so that you sleep like a baby. You stay in one place all night, trapping all that delightful warmth around you, and the weight keeps you from moving in any direction so whatever position you settle into upon retiring will be the same position in which you awake. It is the most restful of sleeps you may ever experience, thanks to the lovely British duvet.

Even the most wonderful things in life come with challenges, which brings me back to my aforementioned sweaty and exhausted condition. You see, the duvet has a cover on it for hygienic purposes and needs to be changed at the same time as the sheets and pillow slips. The removal of the duvet cover is not too difficult. However, reinserting the feather mattress, which is frequently double-wide in size, back into the clean cover—well, that is a different kettle of fish! It is rather like trying to STUFF A CLOUD INTO A CONDOM! You get one corner in and pull, then the other corner comes out! You pull from the bottom, and the top slides south! All the while, you try to find the best position in which to stuff—the bottom of the bed, or standing on the bed and pushing the duvet down, or running next door and seeking help from a neighbor as it is a two-person job for most Americans. I have had all kinds of instructions, as found on the Internet, from my neighbors, and the kind people at the laundry. But the task remains outside of my skill level! Why must everything be so complicated here. Can't they just invent disposable duvets! This seems like such a waste of an afternoon.

However, I do receive the best night's sleep ever, so the payback is worth the exhaustion. But I am on the net in search of black duvet covers so they don't need to be changed so often. Surely there are other people out there who are duvet challenged! In the meantime, I will carry on becoming the typical British housewife and change my duvet cover on a rainy day, which gives me extra time to enjoy an extended nap in a clean bed.

"Without enough sleep, we all become tall two-year-olds." ~ JoJo Jensen

Distractions

During my third summer in the UK, I took a trip to France to visit Chartres Cathedral. I have tried to travel to a different country on every yearly sojourn, in an effort to see as much of Europe as possible. I had heard of the beautiful cathedral and its ancient labyrinth many times in my study of labyrinth history and was anxious to put my feet upon the stones in this magical place of pilgrimage. I entered the cathedral and was awed by the magnificence of it. After locating its thirteenth-century labyrinth, I attempted to walk the stones numerous times. I followed the circuits for several trials, and was ultimately able to complete the cycle toward the center and back out again. The numerous attempts were not due to getting lost, but that my concentration was broken frequently by the multiple distractions.

At one point, I took it all very personally. How could I have traveled so many miles to put my feet on these ancient stones, only to find my attention pulled in different directions by all the extraneous visual and auditory stimuli? It is NOT FAIR, I thought (at which time I could hear my mother's voice saying, "Life is not always fair."). In my dreams of this moment, the cathedral was always eerily quiet, subdued in color, and the only others around were the ghosts of the millions of previous pilgrims throughout the centuries. It was to be a tranquil, personal, yet evocative experience.

What were the distractions that were so bothersome, you ask? Well, the tour buses were timed approximately every thirty minutes, at which time hundreds of lemmings descended upon the labyrinth to reenact a casual form of "hopscotch." Couples attempted to race each other around the circuits to see which could enter the center first. Children bounced around in opposing directions to activate the flashing lights on the soles of their trainers (aka tennis shoes). Avid photographers stood in the middle of the circuits in an attempt to obtain that perfect picture of some obscure artifact on the cathedral ceiling. Women walked with heavy feet in their wooden clogs, creating an echoic din that could be heard throughout the cathedral. Some people even walked while humming, chatting about the weather, or even worse—talking on their cell phones! Phones were ringing, cameras were flashing, translators were speaking in tongues, unwashed travelers were putrefying the air, people were continually cutting across the labyrinth in an effort to find the "way out"—it was all just too much!

Ultimately, I wondered if the point of this experience was,

in fact, all about the distractions. Might this form of chaos be what the Lord sees as He looks down upon the earth? No wonder He has trouble getting our attention. And, equally as astonishing, how can we expect to discern His presence among all the interferences? Do you suppose there are times when He wished He could just tell us to stop the noise, slow down the pace, and concentrate on loving one another? Or, are the distractions of this world necessary to help us focus, to concentrate on that which is most pertinent, thereby discarding all the fluff? Possibly there have always been distractions, although certainly not of the magnitude present today. Conceivably, our goal may be to filter the intrusions, centering on the basic peace God has offered us and ignoring the extraneous provocations that are not conducive to the ultimate journey.

"The labyrinth literally reintroduces the experience of walking a clearly defined path. This reminds us that there is a path, a process that brings us to unity, to the center of our beings. In this simple act of walking, the soul finds solace and peace." ~ Lauren Artress

E
Elders and Escalators

Elder Lunch

One Sunday I had the privilege of being invited to brunch with Dee, my village buddy who took me to church each week, and a few other women from our congregation. These lovely ladies included Nora at one hundred and one years old; Ruby at one hundred; Nancy at ninety-eight, and Ilene, a spring chick at eighty-eight. Annie was in her seventies, as was Dee, and I was the baby of the group at sixty-five. We would leave right after the 10:30 church service and drive to a most impressive restaurant and carvery at the Broadway Golf Course. It is located upon a mesa and overlooks the Cotswold rolling hills. One can see for miles, including at least six villages, sheep pastures, and flowering fields, making a delightful visual quilt. It was a feast for both eyes and palate.

Lunch with these marvelous ladies was a treat. As one can imagine, hearing was an issue, especially since the golfers chose to have their awards ceremony during our meal. Each conversation was an adventure, and the questions and answers never matched. Dee and I got several chuckles.

First, we started with a bottle of wine. The ladies would take turns buying the bottle, and each glass was carefully filled so as to use up exactly that. (In fact, when I joined the group there was some concern of how much I would be drinking so as not to exceed the limit of one bottle.) After several sips of wine, the ladies became quite giddy and it was increasingly more difficult for them to order their meal. When a full meal eventually arrived, those tiny little birds began to devour it with a gusto worthy of a group of truck drivers. It was amazing how much they packed away. After they had cleaned their plates, one of them removed plastic containers from her purse and sent them back to the kitchen to fill for a subsequent meal. It seems they are regulars at the Golf Club and get all kinds of special treatments. What a crack-up!

After dinner they complained of being so full they "couldn't eat another bite." But since dessert is included in the price they proceeded to order their sweets and coffee. They cleaned their plates again. One lady was very concerned about leaving any coffee in the pots and I hoped she would not ask for it to go. As we stood up, Ruby grabbed a leftover pat of butter to take home. Thankfully, it was foil wrapped.

It took slightly longer to get them into the car after the meal than when we first picked them up. Subsequently, there was the stowing of frames, canes, purses, and food containers as well. Over the course of my years in the UK, we have lost three of these wonderful women and the Golf Course is closed to outsiders. I continue to hold them in my memory and marvel at their stamina. I am always amazed at the longevity of life here in the Cotswolds. I don't know whether to attribute it to the water or the wine. My only stress is making sure I drink enough of the local liquids.

"The best classroom in the world is at the feet of an elderly person." ~ Andy Rooney

Centenarian Nora

I first met Nora, one of marvelous brunch companions, after a Good Friday service. I was especially looking forward to church that day, as it had been a while since I had attended a Good Friday service. It was also an opportunity to meet the Reverend Rose. I had spoken with Rose on the phone after the first year I'd arrived, and she had been kind enough to connect me with a ride to the Methodist Church just outside my village.

I had read Reverend Rose's "April Reflection" in the church bulletin from the week prior. I was so impressed with her writing and knew I would also be inspired by her sermon. I was not disappointed. Reverend Rose is a knowledgeable, charming, and charismatic leader. Her sermon was poignant, encompassing all the emotions surrounding Christ's death. It brought back memories of the Passion Play I witnessed in Oberammergau, Germany in 2010. Somewhere in the background of the reading from the Scriptures, I could hear the pounding of nails, jeering of the crowd, belittling of the guards, and weeping of the Marys.

At the end of the service, Dee (my friendly chauffeur) introduced me to Miss Nora, who was sitting across the aisle from me. Nora was a vision in her tweed suit, nylons, heels with matching purse and earrings. I felt quite underdressed in comparison. Her beautiful gray hair had been recently styled with just enough back-combing to give her a little height, bringing her stature to nearly five feet. She immediately welcomed me and asked from whence I'd come. Dee shared that Nora had recently had a birthday. In my head I was calculating somewhere between eighty-five and ninety, but she smiled radiantly and revealed an unbelievable age of one hundred and one! I could not believe it. It was my first exposure to a centenarian, but Nora was not at all what I would have expected. She was sharp as a tack, dressed to the nines, and every bit as lovely as her years of experience would suggest. After a brief conversation, I asked if I could escort her next door to Webb Hall for coffee and hot cross buns. Well, little Nora would not accept my arm, but manipulated the stairs with more grace than my new titanium knees could muster.

As we entered the Hall, it was difficult to say who generated more attention from the elderly gents, Nora or myself. To avoid bedlam, Nora and I graciously sat together and let the gents gather round us. What a delightful time we had. All that attentiveness—well, it was enough to rosy both our cheeks. The menfolk were volleying questions back and forth and Nora and I had a grand old time fielding them.

Alas, it was time for Nora to go and her chauffeur arrived at her elbow. His age I guessed at ninety, but then I had been wrong before. We bid each other adieu and looked forward to seeing each other on Easter Sunday. I then proceeded around the Hall, meeting the other parishioners.

Suddenly all joy of that Good Friday gathering collapsed when Reverend Rose appeared at the door and reported Nora had fallen as she was getting into the car. Someone called for emergency services, while the others, ashen-faced raced to the doors to assess the damage. My heart stopped. Could someone enter your life so briefly, make such an indelible impression, and then be gone? When I got outside, there was Nora, sitting in the front seat of the car. She was covered with dried cypress leaves but smiling blissfully to her audience and telling everyone she thought she was just fine. There was a lot of hubbub from that point on until the emergency service arrived. To be on the safe side they took her on to hospital, with her daughter and son-in-law, who had also been summoned, following close behind.

After returning to our various homes, we waited impatiently to hear word of Nora's condition. Remarkably, she returned home that night to her own bed. I had no doubt that Nora would be in church for Easter Sunday in her finest attire with matching accessories. What an absolute privilege it was to become acquainted with this remarkable woman. Nora lived several more years and never failed to impress me with her wisdom.

> *"When I stand before God at the end of my life, I would hope that I would have not a single bit of talent left and could say, 'I used everything you gave me.'"*
> *~ Erma Bombeck*

Escalator Ups and Downs

My first summer in the UK I left my little village for a while to visit the Fjords of Norway. I walked to the Town Hall to catch a bus, then a train to London Paddington, a taxi to London St. Pancras, a train to Dover, and a taxi to the hotel. The next day, it was another taxi to the cruise ship terminal, where I boarded the Holland America Ryndam, my home for the next seven days. We cruised the Fjords, from Dover to Oslo, Kristiansand, Stavenger and Ulvic before heading back. The scenery was majestic, the cabin was luxurious, the food was delectable, and the service was amazing. Norway reminded me a lot of Alaska, only less snow on their mountains, probably due to the unending rain Europe and England has had for months. It was a lovely vacation from my UK vacation. The most memorable part of the trip was the comfortable bed I had onboard versus the pull-out couch in my studio apartment back in the village. Why did I think I could survive a studio apartment for four months when I live in a four-bedroom house in California?

When the ship docked back in Dover, it was time to reverse the order of the trip—a taxi from the cruise terminal to the train station; the train to London St. Pancras; a taxi to London Paddington; train to Moreton-in-Marsh; bus back to my village; and, finally, the walk back to my abode. Well you can't say I missed many modes of transportation, except bicycle or plane. And I did all this on my own with my backpack, and small suitcase, as well as my camera, sunglasses, cell phone, and umbrella hanging from my belt. I must have looked like a one of those people on expedition. You have to be inventive when traveling on your own.

By the time I got to Paddington Station, I was feeling a bit boastful of my experience thus far. When I came to the elevator or escalator decision to get to the platform, I thought I could handle anything. You guessed it; I chose the escalator. Well, I was only five feet from the bottom when my suitcase shifted and hit the back of my knees. I overcompensated in balance due to my heavy backpack and the next thing I knew, I was moving toward the last two feet of the steps on my back, eyes cast toward the ceiling of the terminal. I looked like a turtle on its shell (aka my backpack) and was unable to even sit up as I slid onto the floor. I no doubt would have been trampled by the passengers behind me had two men with arms the size of tree trunks not lifted me up to an erect position. I couldn't believe I could stand upright, let alone be able to walk. As it turned out, the escalator had not fared as well. I was wearing my glasses on top of my head (a bad habit, I know), and during the fall they flew off and landed under me, becoming wedged into the tiny slits of the stairs. The escalator's downward progress halted, and engineers were called to ascertain the severity of the damage. As if I wasn't embarrassed enough! They wanted me to wait, not to see if I was injured, but to see if the damage to the escalator was "fixable." At this point, I was more worried about having to pay for the damage than any injury I might have incurred to my body. I glanced anxiously at the crowd that was forming all around me, then quickly reached over and pulled the eyeglasses from the escalator steps. The downward movement restarted, and I exhaled a huge sigh of relief.

Eventually I was released by the "escalator police," free to find a chair and regain a sense of composure and dignity. Luckily, after two days of ibuprofen I was almost as good as new (the bruise on my bum cheek faded with time!).

There you have it. Once more Marilyn has been rammed from behind by a wild animal and gone from vertical to horizontal position in three seconds flat. The first time I was pushed down by a male sheep in the pasture; the second, by a Samsonite on the escalator stairs. Now I know why the station shared its name with the chunky Paddington Bear. One must have extra padding to survive a sudden fall.

It wasn't until I got home and changed my clothing that I noticed the telltale escalator black ridges on the backside of my pants. I wonder how many people from London to my village saw me from behind and guessed where my bum had been?

The very next year, I suffered another downward spiral on a Paris escalator. And that, my friends, was the last of my escalator incidents while traveling with luggage. I now join the queue for the lift (aka elevator) with all the other seniors. It takes a little longer, but is well-worth the ultimate wear and tear on the body.

"There was a power outage at a department store yesterday. Twenty people were trapped on the escalators."
~ Steven Wright

F
Forks, Fish, and Fickle Friends

Forks and Knives

Upon my return to England I found myself facing the age-old dilemma of using the fork. In America, we typically use the fork in the right hand (if one is right-handed) with the tines pointing up so as to maximize the shoveling power. The knife sits comfortably at the side of one's plate, waiting patiently to be called upon for its job of either spreading or cutting one's food (as we "colonists" rarely set the table with a spreader and a cutter).

I recall on one particular occasion entering the dining area of a restaurant and immediately being bombarded with the overuse of cutlery. The lights were reflecting off all the silver as diners positioned to enjoy their meal with fork in one hand (usually the left) and knife in the other. And then the fun began, with everyone cutting, stacking and cleaning the edge of his/her knife onto the fork. It was truly a work of art when finished, with a neat, clean knife and a down-turned fork ready for entry, yet I couldn't help thinking that the trajectory seemed all wrong. It would appear the fork's design would be best utilized with the tines turned upward, thereby holding the food within the "scoop" of the bowl shape. Instead, the proper Anglophile piled, pushed, and stuffed his tines with the fork turned downward, looking as though it would all fall off again. But wait! Upon closer inspection, I realized that the eater then approaches the fork (versus the fork approaching the eater in the USA) and immediately snatches each and every morsel without incident.

In America, one typically rests his/her fork on the plate between bites (so as to avoid the "stuffing" of food), and reenters the conversation between bites. (Of course, there is always the commoner who never stops eating or talking, thereby putting the person across the table from him/her in harm's way!). But the proud Englishman stays at the ready between bites by holding both knife and fork in position for the next slice, stab, stack maneuver.

"How hard can it be?" I ask myself. Well, for one thing, I rarely use my left hand; in fact, I've often wondered about the functionality of having two hands when clearly I can only use one of them. I always felt it was just for physical symmetry and/or balance. And now I know! As I approach my fork, held majestically in my left hand, all neatly piled and stacked, I immediately thrust the down-turned tines into my lower lip. Imagine my surprise when the dining room all turned in sync to stare at the novice who just shouted, "Ow!" and had a fork permanently attached to her lower lip! Practice makes perfect, so they say, so all I could do was hope and pray I'd be adept at this maneuver within the next six months.

Ahh, there is even more. When dessert comes, you are given a fork and a dessert spoon. According to my observations, the spoon/fork combo is used in the same complementary fashion as the fork/knife. Quite honestly, I never did figure out whether you push the dessert onto the spoon with the fork or vice versa. Perhaps it has to do with the texture of the pudding. It's all such a challenge to look somewhat knowledgeable about the function of eating with utensils in this country. I shall "relish" the opportunity and lose weight!

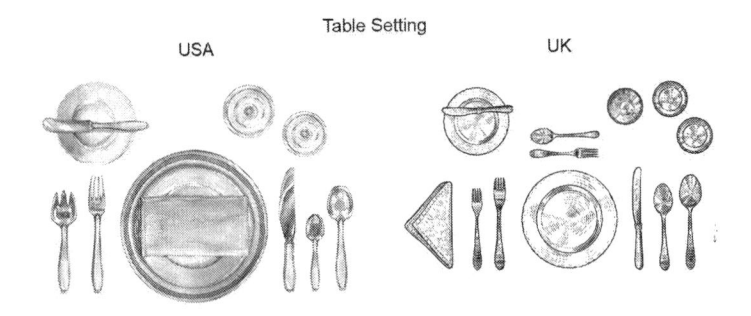

Table Setting
USA   UK

"Is it progress if a cannibal uses a knife and fork?"
~ Stanislaw Jerzy Lec

Gone Fishing

You know it's Friday in the village when the little red van pulls into the Lane. Fred the Fishmonger drives from village to village selling fish fillets fresh from Grimsby, a seaport in Lincolnshire. My nose is more sensitive than the average local on the Lane and, unfortunately, I can smell his wares before he leaves the High Street. I really don't like smell of fish! But I would go out just to have a chat with Fred and stand in the line behind the van and listen to the gossip. On occasion, Lady Jean would ask me to purchase her some fish, so I didn't have to make up an excuse to join the queue.

Fred is a positively delightful chap. True to British style, he's a wonderful conversationalist. He could tell you the history of the fishing industry and beautiful places to visit on the Seacoast, as well as the best piece of fish to buy and how to cook it. Over the eight summers I have lived in the village, I have come to know Fred as the most agreeable of fellows, who is kind to everyone on his route.

Don and Paula have lived in the village most of their lives.

They made sure there was always a parking place for Fred to sell his fish. Don would help Fred set up, then take his place in the queue to have his fish order filled for the week. During that time, Paula would refill Fred's flask with tea and pack up a snack with which to send him on his journey. Between these three wonderful people, the fish business has thrived in our area. This past year, Fred retired from the Fish Van after thirty-three years. Before he passed the rod over to a new "monger," he sang the praises of the delightful Don and Paula, who have taken care of him over the years and treated him like family. What a delight to get to know these wonderful people who are a part of the village's history.

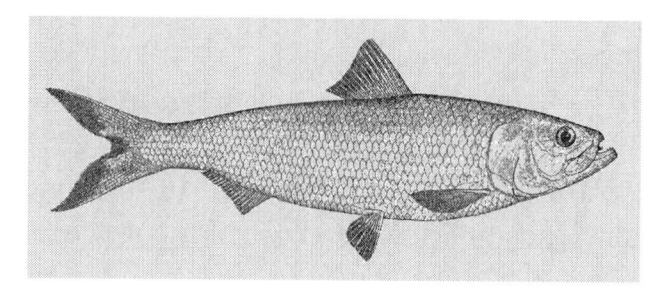

"Child, there's a sayin' every fishmonger has. 'When you buy land, you buy stones. When you buy fish, you buy bones.'" ~ Karen Cecil Smith

Fickle Friends

A sad day it was when I lost my new best friend Mabel. She had been with me ever since I moved into my cottage in June and we had shared secrets as well as lies. That's what good friends do! Alas, Mabel chose to live in the bathroom, while I spent most of my evening hours in the adjoining bedroom. That way, we each had our own space. She liked a little hidey-hole in the crevices of the skylight over the tub-shower.

At first, she was somewhat coy and embarrassed when I took a shower. However, in time, I would see one leg at a time slowly emerge from her hole. However, while washing my hair, shaving my legs, et cetera it became increasingly difficult to manoeuvre and keep one eye on Mabel. (Due to my arachnophobia, our cohabitation was conditioned on her maintaining a healthy distance from me.)

Well, as you can imagine, Mabel steadily developed a cheeky attitude and began playing games with me, like "how close is too close." There were occasional shouting matches (well, the shouting was rather one-sided) as to where the line of demarcation should be drawn.

One morning I awoke with an itching on my bum after my early toilette and discovered a spider bite. Did Mable actually crawl over to the bathroom door where my pajamas were hanging and take up residence? Even more frightening, had she entered the sacred space of the toilet bowl? Just as I flushed, I noticed a black dot circling the bowl. Could it be? Oh, poor Mabel! I was becoming increasingly cross with her, but I didn't wish her harm. Nor did I wish her demise to be so distasteful. I turned on the light and watched the last of her lovely eight legs swirl and disappear from existence

MORAL OF THIS STORY: Don't bite the bum that keeps you.

G
Glorious Gardens and Guilty Pleasures

Gardens Everywhere

One of my favorite movies is *Howards End*, with Anthony Hopkins, Emma Thompson, and Vanessa Redgrave. I could watch the introductory scene over and over, as Vanessa Redgrave takes a stroll amidst her garden in her country estate. She wears a purple dress with a long train that rustles in the long grass as she walks. She brushes the flowers, emitting a floral scent that you can almost smell coming from the screen.

That's what it is like when strolling through the Open Gardens in my village. Almost thirty homes open their gardens one weekend during the summer to the public. We gawk, ask questions, take pictures, and take in the wonderful scents. The gardens vary in design, size, and shape, but the flowers are very similar. Rhododendrons, roses, peonies, lupine, poppies, foxgloves, and irises are in full color and standing at attention for the casual gardener to drool at with envy. The foliage of various hues complements the colors of the flowers.

The garden layouts and design elements seem to capture the personalities of the home/estate owners. Some were frenzied in their initial preparation; somewhat like throwing a handful of seeds from one's front porch and letting it come up wherever it landed. Others have a hand-trimmed look, giving away the handiwork of a professional gardener. Others plant a series of gardens—one for patio dining, one for the children's play yard, and one for sitting and watching the sunset or feeding the birds. The "art objects" among the flowering beds also reflect the tastes of the homeowner. One, I recall, contained a large ceramic pig lolling on the grass, another planted an airplane engine among the foliage, and many had various art sculptures carefully placed to draw your eye. Most include the rose garland archway, which was lovely to look at, but dangerous to stroll under due to thorny branches catching on your clothing or dangers of meeting a bevy of bees.

Some of the owners are in their gardens to tell you the names of various plants, give you a history on their cottage, or just to enjoy conversation with fellow horticulturists. The serious looky-loos make mental notes on how to reconstruct their own gardens when they return home. The rest of us merely thank the homeowner for opening their gardens for our enjoyment. All have a delightful time wandering the village in search of the next open garden to "ooh" and "aah." And, in true English fashion, there are stops for tea strategically placed along the route. One could not ask for better entertainment for the weekend.

Looking across the landscapes, the cottage roofs are a mixture of slate or thatch, but all gardens are typically walled with the Cotswold yellow stone. Although we cannot get close enough to peer in windows, one could imagine the inside of the various cottages by the state of their gardens. Many also have additional kitchen gardens, filled with vegetables, herbs, and fruit trees. It seems the staples are still grown at home if there is a plot big enough to put in a few plants. The English enjoy their fresh vegetables all summer long, reminding one of the allotments planted throughout history.

"To plant a garden is to believe in tomorrow." ~ Audrey Hepburn

Going on a "Guilt" Trip

You wonder as you plan for a trip away from home what you will be missing. Will you have regrets about something you neglected? If someone gets sick, will you be torn about whether to leave and go home? One doesn't wish for those thoughts to enter their mind, but they do—at least they did for me. I have a disease called "guilt" that creeps into my psyche from time to time and spoils a perfectly good conscience. Goodness knows I fight the disease from every front. I even checked on a possible inoculation before leaving home, but to no avail. One year for Christmas, my children gave me a pin that said, "My mother is a travel agent for guilt trips."

And so, it goes! Two events came up within the first three months of my trip overseas. First my mum in the States had emergency gallbladder surgery. Two procedures were needed before she was done, which took its toll on her strength.

We luckily had contingency plans in place, and they worked wonderfully. My brother was notified and he in turn told my roommate, who was at the hospital before the ambulance arrived. Both my kids were there before she went to surgery and were subsequently helpful in getting Mum settled and on the road to recovery. She was transferred from the hospital to the Health Care unit at her retirement village, where she continued to receive physical therapy until she was able to be on her own in her apartment. You plan for these things, but you never want to test them out. As well, I always feel I need to be the one in my family to care for everyone. Behold! I was not needed. I don't know which hit me worse—guilt for being away, or not being needed. I plan, God smiles!

The second story concerns my brother and his beautiful partner, who at the time had been together for almost twenty-five years. The family had suggested marriage on numerous occasions, but for whatever reason they never heeded our advice. Instead, they waited until I was five time zones away to decide "now is the time." They chose a quiet ceremony with two witnesses, which would not have included me even if I were home, but that is all beside the point. I hurriedly ordered flowers, tried to put my congratulations on paper to them, and sent off a card. Even the card choice was difficult. Should it be a wedding card or a Silver Anniversary card? Either way, I would not be able to be there. Guilt strikes again!

So, there it is. My fears came to fruition, just as I knew they would. What I did not anticipate was how quickly the feelings of guilt and remorse went away. In fact, a good walk and a cup of tea were all it took to let it go. It helped, of course, that my mother did very well in her recuperation, and I wasn't even invited to my brother's wedding. The point I am making is that I was able to cope with it all. The question remains, am I finally getting a handle on some of my negative feelings? Or, does distance simply make the heart grow harder?

"Life is what happens to us while we are making other plans." ~ Allen Saunders

H
Hymns to Hedgehogs

Hymns to Sing

I really love the people in my Methodist Church in the UK (all fourteen of them). They have taken up residence in my heart. The Reverend Rose usually only attends the first Sunday of the month; in between, we have local preachers and elders who officiate the services. Some are very good, but none of them compete with Rose. For instance, one week a delightful pastor officiated, but his deliverance was so slow that I wished for a wind-up key on his back. My guess is his ten-minute sermon was extended to twenty-five just by pacing his pauses. On the other hand, how long do you want to preach on the beheading of John the Baptist?

No matter who preaches the sermon, we will sing a minimum of five hymns during the service, most with seven verses each. The Methodist hymnal is filled with old favorites written by John Wesley and Isaac Watts, to name a few, from those glorious 1700s. It's not the words to these oldies, but goodies I mind, but the music. It resembles a slide up and down the scale, feeling much like the sea ebbing and flowing. The hymnals only have the words, so we must rely on the organ music for the tune. Consequently, the first verse is usually pretty quiet while everyone adjusts to the tune and tempo. The old musicians must have had much larger ranges when they sang, as the music varies from mezzo-soprano to bass within one verse, making it almost impossible to sing all the way through without some lip-synching. If the hymn has seven verses, we sing all seven. No skipping verses in the English Methodist Church. Time seems to be negotiable in England, except for the bus and trains.

We have sung "Amazing Grace" and "The Church is One Foundation," which were the only two hymns I recognize as the same tune over time. It does make me appreciate my California church and our modern choir director, who presents a variety of lovely works by composers from the twentieth and twenty-first centuries. It has also been difficult to get used to just congregation singing versus having a choir. Of course, with only fourteen in the congregation, they *are* the choir!

One cannot speak of church music without making reference to the organ. Only one among us is able to play the organ full time; therefore for many years they had a versatile music machine that can be played like a keyboard, or insert discs to correspond with hymn of choice. So how did they get all those hymns of the 1700s on computer discs? Did they bring Wesley back to record them? It is a wonder.

"Those who wish to sing always find a song." ~ Swedish Proverb

The Hunt for the Elusive Hedgehog

One of my favorite evening pastimes is to hunt for hedgehogs. What delightful creatures! English hedgehogs coats are made of stiff, sharp spines and if attacked they turn into a prickly and unappetizing ball that deters most predators. During the daytime, they stay in their protective ball and hidden. However, in the evening, they venture about foraging for food.

The best time to see them is in the early morning hours before the world comes to life and all is still quiet. You will find them moving around the garden with their wobbly gait, being ever so cute. They dart in and out of the foliage as if they were kings or queens of their domains. Unfortunately, I have never actually seen any of the babies, but it's on my bucket list.

One day while gardening my friends found an adult hedgehog hiding in a drain pipe. This was a real treat for me to see. They can ball up into the smallest diameter imaginable, considering their actual size. Handling requires gloves, of course.

These lovely creatures are popular subjects for the children's book author or card maker in the UK. I have a favorite card illustrator in my village that keeps me in abundant supply.

"We all make mistakes, as the hedgehog said as he climbed off the scrubbing brush." ~ Anne Sullivan Macy

I
Idyllic Iona

The Trek to Iona

I had been introduced to the labyrinth by my friend Al in San Diego. I was fascinated by the energy of "walking the path" and anxious to learn more about it. When a Labyrinth Facilitator training became available in August of 2015, I jumped at the chance. After all, I was already in the UK. How far could a trip to Scotland be for this seasoned traveler? The training was located on the Isle of Iona, a small island on the West coast of Scotland in the Inner Hebrides. The Abbey on Iona has been the center of Gaelic monasticism for three centuries. Today the Island is known as a place of spiritual tranquility and the home of many spiritual retreats.

As I began researching the area, I realized the trip itself was about to be a "pilgrimage" of sorts. The actual trip would encompass two days of travel each way in order to allow for all the train, bus, and ferry schedules. This did not daunt my enthusiasm during the planning period; however, the reality of meeting all the time schedules was indeed overwhelming. I truly kissed the ground at Iona when I arrived.

The trek began in my village by taking a bus to the nearest train station. From there, I changed trains in Oxford, Edinburgh, Glasgow Queen Street, and embarked in Oban. To meet the timetables for the ferry out of Oban, I spent the night. Then it was up early to catch the ferry from Oban to Craigmure on the Isle of Mull. A local bus took me across Mull to another ferry in Fionnphort. I crossed the inlet for a fifteen-minute ferry to dock in Iona. On a clear day, Iona is visible for almost the entire ferry ride, with its beautiful Abbey sitting centerstage. The actual Isle of Iona is just over a mile wide and five miles long, which one would walk over the course of the week's retreat. So just to recap the journey, that was two buses, four trains, two ferries, two taxis and an overnight stay. To say I was exhausted before the training even started was no exaggeration; however, the scenery was breathtaking, especially the Lochs from Glasgow North and the countryside across Mull.

And the week retreat began. Days of walking a cloth labyrinth laid down in the Visitor's Center, an ancient rock labyrinth in the pasture, and making labyrinths on the beach. We strolled the island, attended service in the Abbey, prayed in the Cloisters, danced in the ruins of the Nunnery, and visited with the local wildlife including sheep, goats, Highland Cows (pronounced "Heila Coos"), and ghastly insects called "midges," which would cover any exposed skin with bites in a nano-second. It was a most incredible experience—once in a life-time, and well worth the trip!

Before I knew it, it was time to retrace my journey back to the Cotswolds—ferry to Fionnphort, bus across Mull, ferry to Oban, trains to Glasgow, Wolverhampton, and on to Oxford. Then I experienced a glitch—some trouble on the train line that caused a wait in Oxford for about two hours. By the time I deboarded there were no taxis available at my local station. Luckily there was a woman on the train who had left her car at the station and gave me a ride back to my village around midnight. Not exactly a time to try hitchhiking with luggage! All the way home, I could hear my Mum's words of warning in accepting a ride from a stranger as a surefire path to "dead in a ditch." But I was so full of trust and love from Iona, I could feel no fear. Since that magical trip I have walked many labyrinths in many significant cities, but nothing compares to the comradery and centering around the labyrinth we made on the beach in Iona.

Beach Labyrinth

It's nearing the end of the day,
The sky is beginning to darken,
Yet the sand is still warm from the afternoon sun.
The kelp is glimmering from its temporary beach home;
The sand labyrinth is calling to me.

My walking stick serves as a staff,
To sketch the classic pattern of the labyrinth,
Initiated with the cross.
The heart of our pilgrimage and
The journey of our time together.

The seed pattern is drawn.
We look to the sea and begin connecting the dots
To form the circuits.
The display scrolls across the sand,
Flowing like the tide of the sea.

At last the pattern is complete.
Together hands gather precious seaweed, sticks, and shells,
All gifts from the beach.
And we outline the path that will guide us to the center.

We join hands to envelope this sacred space,
Embodying those precious gifts of the sea.
And we say a blessing for these treasures
And presence of each other,
On the bay of Martyrs at the edge of Iona.

A rainbow greets us, pointing the way to Mull,
And we enter the labyrinth.
Each at our own pace, alone with our thoughts,
Yet clinging to our connection to each other,
Much like the sand adheres to the soles of our feet.

As the sun begins to set,
So does our journey begin to close.
We all celebrate in the fuchsia coloring of the sky,
Radiating across the West,
Drawing us to our far away homes.

And a full moon shows itself,
In magnificent splendor,
As we peacefully slip away into slumber,
Bidding farewell to our Iona.
Till we meet again.

~ Marilyn Honea, 2015

"Walk as though you are kissing the earth with your feet." ~ *Thich Nhat Hanh, Buddhist Monk*

J
Jackdaws

Jackdaws in the Treetops

My first abode in the UK was a lovely three-story house, with the bedroom in the upper floor and a view of the treetops. One spring morning, I awoke to some lovely chirping from the budding limbs outside my bedroom window. It was a most welcome sound, almost as though the darling visitors were coaxing me to "wake up and enjoy the day." Sweet chirps to softly bring one to wakeful consciousness.

About the time I had finished with my shower, the doves had taken over the trees outside my bedroom. I'd always thought their coos were somewhat melodic and soothing; I will say, however, that when they sing "in mass" they become somewhat obnoxious. These arias were constant, one could set the clock to them each day. No wonder the dovecotes were located in the barns in the days of yore.

Then, as nighttime drew nearer, a black flying nuisance would enter the picture. It started as just one, then two, then thirty. The famous "jackdaw" has arrived. Spring, I realize, is mating season for the jackdaw and there is a constant discourse that takes place between the male and female of the species. If you listen carefully, you can almost hear the conversations. Molly and Ethel are discussing the finer points of the mating ritual. "Those men are just oversexed. Can't they think of something else to talk about?" Rita, who is still in her hibernating phase, is also complaining about being too tired and suffering from a migraine (pronounced "MEE gran" by the English Jackdaw). Eddy flits from branch to branch hoping to sneak up on some unsuspecting female who has turned her back to his approach. All at once, Eddy lets out a "gotcha" and the whole covey starts to scream "intruder" and they fly in mass toward another tree. And then the dialogue begins all over again. This goes on every four to five minutes from tree to tree from dusk to sundown. Then they all simply agree to the fact that it is much too difficult to locate any black bird in the dark. Ah, if Eddy only had some reflective Nikes, he could "just do it."

Such was the daily symphony in the springtime outside my rooftop sanctuary. How could one possibly miss weekly choir rehearsal when they listen daily to a full symphony of voices. I had certainly noticed the birds back home—the mockingbirds, owls, ravens, hawks, and our resident falcon, which made more "noise" than music—but had never been treated to such performances. Or possibly it was just that in my treetop home I felt like an intruder in their world and tried to be somewhat more tolerant. At any rate, it was very nice to be such a part of nature that they became my daily reminders of time and community.

I would miss seeing the winged creatures when the trees were all leafy in summer. For the moment, however, as we observed each other, them from the barren tree limbs and I through my window, I couldn't help but wonder what they were saying about me. "Man, what a life, wrapped up in a lovely warm duvet with not a care in the world." Or possibly, "Sure am glad I don't have to carry all her burdens. Even that duvet looks cumbersome. I'm glad I can generate my own warmth."

These are just some of my musings on those mornings when I scrunched down in my warm coverlet and tried for an extra half hour of snoozing before the next choral response began. It's a bit like nodding off in church. Just when you are about to pitch forward in the pew, the choir breaks out in song to keep you in your seat and save the embarrassment of discovery.

"The swans will not sing till the jackdaws are quiet."
~ Unknown

K
Kitchen Electrics

Kitchen Manuals and Electrics

I have stayed at several Holiday Lets (cottages) over the course of my eight summers in the UK. One of the first things I do when entering my new abode is to look for the notebook which contains all the appliance manuals. Don't expect to know exactly how to work the fridge, microwave, stove, washer/dryer without additional explanation. Although these may be plugged into the wall socket, there is an additional on/off switch with every socket. It took me several months to remember to use these switches with small appliances, such as the toaster or hotpot, without checking to see that the power switch is on. The burners on the stovetop are usually electric, and may heat much differently from your cooktop at home. Ovens are gauged by "marks" as opposed to "degrees." UK power is around 230V, so 110 appliances brought from home (except electronics) may be rendered unusable from their very first plug-in. Additionally, the plugs are three-pronged and will not accept any two-prone plug from the US.

Then there is the matter of the refrigerator (I use this term loosely, as most "fridges" fit under the counter. That means bending at the waist to retrieve any ice cubes in the freezer (the size of a glove box in a US auto). The milk/juice require further bending south. And one must lie on their stomach to reach the crisper drawers that are typically at the bottom.

If you are lucky enough to acquire a cottage with a full-size fridge, it will still look miniature next to the fridges in the US.

Washer/dryer combinations also vary in their configuration and instructional information. It still baffles me how you can wash, then dry, in the same machine! Weren't we always warned about water and electricity not mixing? The dryers are not readily designed for anything but cotton, so often you hang many of your polyester and nylon articles on hangers all around the house. At any given moment when someone knocks on the door, be ready to grab your knickers out of sight if they are near the door.

If you are so unlucky to blow the circuit breaker by plugging in two appliances at once, it is always best to secure the location of the circuit box with the property owner on your first walk-through. The British love to hide these necessary items in the most unusual places at any location throughout the cottage.

There are some things in a kitchen one must just learn to live with (or without, depending). My last year there I asked my landlord to fix the dripping faucet in the kitchen. The loud droplets falling into the stainless-steel sink was very annoying. He graciously left for the Co-op and returned with a brand-new sponge. He carefully placed the sponge under the drip to absorb the sound and proceeded to explain that I should squeeze it out on occasion. You can lead a landlord to water, but...)

"Never trust a skinny cook." ~ Unknown

L
Lords/Ladies and Liquids

I was invited by nobility to take tea in the House of Lords in London. Can you believe it—this plucky California woman getting an invitation to Parliament? No doubt they wanted my liberal views. At the time President Obama was busy in Ireland with the G8, addressing the Syrian woes, and therefore unavailable for the event, and I was ever so glad to stand in at his absence. My dear friend Jean, the Lady of High Street, was the president of the Women's Council, a charity organization involved in aiding disabled Asian Children and their families. The Tea Party was held in the Cholmondeley Room at the House of Lords. The setting was very posh, the women were lovely, though unfortunately the "tea" would turn out to be a bit disappointing.

Lady Jean, her friend Carolyn, and I caught the noon train from Moreton on Marsh to Paddington. A car met us at the station and took us to the Black Rode Garden Entrance of the House of Lords. We were ushered into the Cholmondeley Room, which was a marquee extension on the terrace. The decor was all pink fabric (an interesting color for Lords). Inside the pink folds of the marquee ceiling hung several lovely chandeliers. The tables were set for eight per table.

The sounds of London were easily discernible outside the marquee from the terrace overlooking the River Thames. The chimes of Big Ben were interspersed with boat noises from the River and the tinkling of spoons stirring in teacups. The views from the terrace were lovely, including The Houses of Parliament, the tower of Lambeth Palace (London home of the Archbishop of Canterbury), Westminster Bridge, and County Hall. A sight quoted by William Wordsworth in 1802 as, "Earth has not anything to show more fair: Dull would he be of soul who could pass by a sight so touching in its majesty." The only blight on the horizon was the London Eye, which in my opinion is more of an "eyesore." It just doesn't fit with the surrounding architecture. I wonder what Wordsworth would have said about that huge Ferris wheel diminishing the view?

The tea included three courses: sandwiches, scones, and sweets. The spread was far more impressive in its presentation than taste, a bit surprising to this tea connoisseur. Although there were cloths on the table, the serviettes (napkins) were paper! They were placed in the middle of the table in what looked like a toast rack, verses at the individual place settings. The triangle sandwiches were tasteless, the sweets were store-bought, and the scones were dry. And there were no serving tongs on the table for the various food items, and needed to be extracted with one's fork or fingers! We even had to ask for more tea to be served. All in all, the teas I present at home are far more appetizing and aesthetically pleasing. On the other hand, the clotted cream was straight from Devon, and divine.

Of course, it wasn't about the "tea" so much as the experience. The women were delightful, from all parts of the world. It resembled a United Nations audience. The day was an overall success and one I will probably not be able to duplicate, unless the Queen asks me for tea in the future. In that case, I will expect homemade pastries, cloth napkins, and someone at my elbow to keep my teacup filled. In the meantime, being a guest at the House of Lords will have to serve as my social high point.

"The House of Lords is a model of how to care for the elderly." ~ Frank Field

So Much Liquid, So Little Time

Regarding one's choice of libation, there is considerable emphasis on the time of day, the temperature, and one's mood. Of course, tea is the drink of choice, but I am noticing more English are drinking a cup of coffee in the morning and again after their dinner hour (which is 8:00 p.m., typically when I crawl into my comforter for warmth). After your choice is made for coffee or tea, then there is the choice of milk, sugar, lemon with tea, as well as cream, sugar, or froth for coffee. Tea usually comes in a pot with an extra pot of hot water. Naturally, the hot water pot comes at the same time as the teapot, so unless you quickly empty both pots, you are faced with tepid water. However, you do get more cups of tea per pound (that's money, not weight) than in the US. On occasion, coffee is served in a lovely French Press, which means at least two cups per serving. But if you order one of those fancy cappuccinos, one cup is all you get. When the weather is wet and cold, the only way to warm your hands is with a hot cup of anything.

The danger of drink, of course, is choosing which accompaniment to have with your beverage. It is very difficult to order either tea or coffee without a delectable sweet to "make the medicine go down." Most establishments have a wide array of tempting treats just inside the door, so you rarely get by with just a cuppa. My favorite is the delectable British scone, served with clotted cream and jam! However, British scones are large and dense and one must be careful how many to consume in a day. My husband used to say, "They may go in as a scone, but they come out as a stone."

When the weather is hot, which it never is in England, there is nothing like a pint of beer. Of interest, wine is also catching on in the UK. Most of the ladies enjoy a lovely glass of Pinot or Merlot with their dinner or for just an outing with their mate to the pub. The choice is to either guzzle or sip. In my opinion, you get more wine for your time, as you tend to sip it longer than downing a pint of lager or pilsner. The advantage to pub drinking is that one concentrates more on the social event than eating. Calorie for calorie, the pub drinks may be the better choice than tea and scones.

There is always one's standing in the community to consider. Let's face it, tea sipping with your pinkie up is much more sophisticated than slugging down a brew. Hot chocolate drinkers, you are out on all counts, as it much too juvenile for an adult in public.

Tea or coffee is available in most any tea shoppe or restaurant. However, the pub is my favorite meeting place on the whole island. In our small village alone, there are more pubs than public conveniences (aka toilets). Pub crawling as soon as one enters a village is essential to finding your comfort zone. The parameters for selection include the Bar Keep, clientele, number of liquid choices, types of bar snacks, and varieties of beer on tap. It staggers the mind to choose only one "favorite" pub. My personal libation after 4:00 p.m. is the gin and tonic. Even better, a G & T with salt and vinegar crisps (that's potato chips in the US). (WARNING: Never eat salt and vinegar crisps with chapped lips!)

The choice of libation is always yours, of course. If you are short on coins, just be sure they don't charge for the loo before you imbibe. Cheers!

"A good local pub has much in common with a church, except that a pub is warmer, and there is more conversation. ~ William Blake

M
Methodists and Music

Methodist Church

My village has a Catholic, Baptist, and Church of England, but no Methodist church, so finding one was on my to-do list that first year. I located a congregation in an adjoining village three miles away and called Reverend Rose, the pastor listed in my local directory (I suppose I should call it a booklet, rather than a directory, as the residential section is all of seven pages and the whole book, including advertisements, is about the size of US restaurant menus.) At any rate, Reverend Rose phoned me back and arranged a call from one of the parishioners. That is how I met Dee. We spoke on the phone and arranged to meet in front of the Chemist building on the High Street (that's pharmacy for those of you who do not speak the Queen's English).

The date change for Daylight Savings is about two weeks later in the UK than in the States. Also important, the clock on a computer does not automatically reset itself unless you change the location in the settings. You can probably see where I am going with this. Between not knowing exactly when the time changed and not having it automatically reset on the computer, I did not arrive at the time we had agreed upon, and Dee was not there when I did. Well, I set out on foot to go to the Baptist church further down on High Street instead. When I arrived at their doors, it was locked. It seems the Baptists have outgrown their church and are now meeting in the local school on Sundays. Without my map handy, I decided to walk back to St. James' Parish, which I had attended the week before. Lo and behold, before I got there, I found the school and joined the Baptists for their worship. Their service was contemporary in nature, which the locals refer to as the "Happy Clappy" service.

Upon arriving home, I had to call Dee and explain my embarrassment over not meeting her on time. She graciously offered to pick me up the following week for Palm Sunday service. It seems they always give Americans a second chance to right themselves.

The Methodist church was constructed of sturdy red brick instead of yellow Cotswold stone (We Methodists like to be obvious in the community so you can spot us easily.) Reverend Rose was not in attendance that morning, but another itinerant preacher was there in her place. As mentioned, the clergy works a circuit of several churches in the area and rotate weekly. For the most part, this is volunteer work and they all are either retired now or work at other jobs during the week. At any rate, I enjoyed a wonderful Palm Sunday sermon and received a cross made of a palm frond. Weeks before, daffodils had been given to me at the Church of England for Mothering Sunday. Now, palm crosses given at the Methodist church. Someone should tell the Baptists that we expect Sunday favors—not just happy, clappy music!

I was given a history of the Methodist Church on that first Sunday of attendance. The chapel met in a private home in 1903. It was described as being "off the road, up the narrowest of paths between hedges, across a brook, nestling in the corner of the greenest of meadows". The initial membership was fourteen individuals. As I looked around the chapel on my first day, I counted fourteen, including the minister and organist. Growth is evidently not an overwhelming concern in this church.

At any rate, the chapel was lovely. The same pew maker was contacted who made the pews in the local C of E (Church of England). However, being comfort conscious, the Methodist installed pads on the bench seats with some occasional pillows for the elderly to prop their backs against. My first question was the nature of the metal plate that was installed where the kneelers are usually found in the C of E church. They looked terribly hard on the knees; however, upon closer inspection, I saw a wire connected at the bottom and realized they were pew heaters. Hallelujah, the Methodists intended a "warmer" reception! Ninety minutes later, however, my legs and feet were no warmer than when I arrived. It seems they had not worked in several years. The only other heating visible were eight heat lamps installed approximately eighteen feet above the pews. It reminded me of the heat lamps in a deli keeping the food warm while waiting for pick-up. We were by no means overdone at the end of the service, in fact, if anything, I felt even colder. (To their credit, the church has since been fitted with radiators in each pew. I do believe my teeth chattering every Sunday helped make this happen.)

The hymnal was copyrighted in 1983 and many of the hymns dated back to the 1800s. The first title I recognized was "All Glory, Laud, and Honor" (pronounced "Aw Gla'way, Lawd, and Hoh'na"). We sang six hymns during the service, including all four to seven verses, which involved a considerable amount of time. But true to the Methodist fashion, it did not cut the pastor's message any shorter (hence the ninety minutes).

The congregation and pastors were most kind, and they apologized that several of their members were on vacation.

(Possibly they should invest in some inflatable people to fill the pews in their absence.) I asked Dee to pick me up for Good Friday and Easter morning services later that week. Dee and I still laugh at me asking for an occasional ride to church, for she was still hauling me around the countryside eight years later!

I was particularly charmed by the bulletin received for the service. It contained a prayer, a pastoral reflection, and a lovely recipe for Malaysian Banana Pancakes with Coconut Lemon Curd. Now that was a find! I made a mental note to email our pastor in the US regarding recipe inserts.

"You know you are a Methodist when...someone says 'May the Force be with you' and you respond, 'And also with you.'" ~ Garrison Keillor

Village Music

There is music everywhere in the village on any given day. It can be as subtle as the birds singing in the garden, the tinkling of teaspoons stirring in a cup, the bleating of the lambs in pasture, live or canned music wafting out of the pub portals, or simply the cacophony of women greeting each other in the

High Street or over the garden fence.

In our village, we hold an annual Music Festival in May—fourteen glorious evenings of classical music from guest performers. One can be entertained by the music of Chopin, Schubert, Haydn, Debussy, Mozart, Beethoven, Brahms, Liszt, Mendelssohn, or Weber. The performers are all exemplary, and each evening is filled with impressive sensory stimulation. During the weekday, university students are given opportunities to "strut their stuff" and include some awesome talent as well. The local school children are able to attend these noontime performances gratis. Each day brings a remarkable opportunity to hear the very best in classical composition.

The evening performances take place in the St. James Church, which affords the best acoustics in the area. I have been privileged to Steward for several seasons. What an honor to be in association with some of the most remarkable performers, greet the elite from surrounding villages, and have an opportunity to give back to my community. A genuine highlight of my summers!

"Music gives a soul to the universe, wings to the mind, flight to the imagination, and life to everything." ~ Plato

N
Naughty and Nice

Naughty Nancy

No matter which pub you frequent, there is the usual character that the locals ignore because they have "heard it all before." In one of my favorite pubs this person is a local lady who we will refer to as Naughy Nancy. She has enough stories to fill her own book. Nancy knows immediately who the newbies are in the pub and hones in on them like a laser beam. Before you know it, the unsuspecting traveler is listening with awe to her narratives and buying her an unsettling amount of beer in hopes of ending her tirade. They should only know that there is no end to Nancy's tales and she could drink even the barman under table. Once in a great while, some good Samaritan will come along and rescue the newbie, thereby cutting off the endless pints that Nancy can consume. In the end, it is a blessing for all concerned!

My favorite anecdote from Nancy is her tale of her mother and father who were both employed in one of our local hotels. In fact, Nancy was conceived in that very hotel adding (in her mind) to the hotel's history. In her words (not mine), "I was born on the wrong side of the sheets." I'll leave that to your own interpretation.

My point in telling you all this? Beware of the one person sitting alone in a pub, for he or she may be watching you and hitting on you for their next beer. That said, if you are open to this experience I can promise you some memorable stories.

"They say many people die because of alcohol. Ironically they never mention how many were born because of it."
~ unknown

Nice and Sweet

Among the residents of any given village, there are those who will always remember you from year to year, ask about your family, and inquire where you are renting this year.

I have found most of these delightful locals running the shops. Without mentioning any names, I must give tribute to the owners of the Co-Op, flower shop, bakery, deli, wine shop, and local gift store. Although I have already spoken of my delightful mail carrier, the post mistress is also one of the most influential residents and always knows your name. Likewise, the librarians are always on hand to greet you by name and may even have book recommendations based on your reading history. I feel a bit like Norm in *Cheers* when I enter the room with these delightful friends.

The same is true whenever I queue at the bus stop, where I always meet an old or new friend. Because I am there so often, travelers think I can answer all questions regarding bus routes, train schedules, and points of interest. Bolstered by this experience, I even inquired about volunteering my time and "expertise" at the village Information Center. Alas, they felt my community knowledge was too limited, but I think it was my American accent that turned them off. Well, their loss. I still give directions, advice, and all around good cheer from the sidewalk.

"If we could eliminate the concept of town and return to live in small villages, all world problems were solved."
~ Rossana Condoleo

O
Olimpicks, Olympics, and Other Oddities

Olimpicks

As mentioned in the tale of my harrowing meeting with the ram, the beginning of June always marks the opening of the Olimpicks in our lovely village. The tradition traces it roots back to 1612, after which it continued, with some discontinuations and reconstructions, until its cancellation in 1852. After nearly a century, however, the games were revitalized by a local, Robert Dover, in 1963. Created in the spirit of inclusion of all classes, "Olimpicks 2.0" are not your typical Greek games of today. A temporary wooden structure, dubbed "The Castle" is erected on a hill which includes a natural amphitheatre. Small cannons are on hand to mark the opening of the games. Some of the events include coursing with hounds, horse racing, jumping, running, sledgehammer throwing, fighting with swords and cudgels, and wrestling. More recently, the games have included tug of war, jousting and fighting, obstacle races, throwing the hammer or shot put, and shinkicking heats. Referred to as the "English martial art," modern-day kicking is done with the combatants stuffing their pants/socks with straw for padding as their opponents attempt to force them to the ground by kicking with the inside of their foot or toe. Is it any wonder that this is my personal favorite?

At the end of the games, torches are lit and attendees descend from the hill and into the town square, lighting up the night and beginning the best and brightest beer brawl. It's only one night of rousing good times and the townspeople put up with the ruckus, as it is all in good fun!

The next day, after the square is cleaned up of its bottles and debris, a lovely parade takes place with floats, a queen and court, bands, Morris Dancers, and lots of food and drink. My personal favorite are the Morris Dancers and the school children dancing around the maypole. The Morris Dancers have been performing folk dancing for over five hundred years. They typically dress in white, with colorful sashes or vests, bells attached to their shins, and dance/jingle to music holding sticks, batons, or kerchiefs. Their routines are intricate, synchronized, and lively. Good times! The whole village turns out for the day and enjoys a wonderful entertainment and amusement rides. It is our village's annual event and not to be missed.

Morris Dancers

"Try everything once except incest and folkdancing."
~ Sir Thomas Beecham

Olympics

The summer of 2012, London sponsored the Olympic Games. It was the year an actor portraying the Queen of England arrived at the Opening Ceremony by parachuting from a helicopter; Jamaican sprinter Usain Bolt won the Gold for 100m and 200m; and American swimmer Michael Phelps won four gold and two silver medals. It was an exciting year to be in the UK. I was able to watch most of the events on my computer, in the comfort of my cottage, without navigating the crowd in London. Even though I missed the grand ceremony and events in person, I was able to participate in some of the local activities.

In the months prior to the Opening Ceremony, every village carried the torch throughout England on its way to London. On July 1st, the flame came down our High Street. People lined the sidewalks, cheered from their stoops, and waved from the upstairs windows. I was able to escort Lady Jean from her front entryway to wave the torch as it passed her domicile. As we waited for the crowd to disperse, she shared the story of her own participation in the Olympics of 1948. Her Ladyship represented her hometown of Torquay in swimming. I have to admit I felt very special seeing the torch pass by in the company of a former Olympian. Truly, I do not make these events up, dear readers. They are just too remarkable not to be true.

"I don't run away from a challenge because I am afraid. Instead, I run toward it because the only way to escape fear is to trample it beneath your feet." ~ Nadia Comaneci, gold-medal gymnast

Oddities

One weekend I had a visit from a friend's daughter who was attending classes in London. What a delight to have a young person visiting my cottage. When exploring the area, I pointed out the former house of the inventor of the Slide Rule. Although this was impressive to me, the bright 20-year-old seemed a bit perplexed. After some thought, she responded with, "Which rule? Was it where you only slide 'down' the slide, not walk 'up' it?". How can a young person seem so innocent and make you feel so old at the same time?

On Sunday, the Vicar of St. Lawrence Church declared during the service, "Covering up a lie is like feeding a pig 'pork pie'". Words to live by, no doubt.

Often in Holiday Lets, they provide a drying rack for one's wet unmentionables. Depending on the layout of the cottage, there never is a good place to put it, as outside is forbidden for the soggy knickers. It does seem no matter where you choose to place the rack for drying in the house, that will always be the room frequented by visitors, workmen, or the occasional stranger.

English beds come in varying sizes as in the US, with one exception. UK bed dimensions include single, double, king, and super king. It seems they have no trouble sleeping on a 'king', but never on a 'queen'!

Methodist joke: "How many Methodists does it take to change a lightbulb?"
Answer: "Change?!"

The term for 'overcast' in the USA is replaced by 'sunny intervals' in the UK.

One hundred years to Americans is similar to 100 miles to the British.

During a sermon in our local church, the pastor quoted the statistic, "If Americans ate 10% less meat apiece, the world would not go hungry." True to British fashion, the pastor then apologized to me personally for picking on Americans.

As I was sitting in a tea shoppe, a Grandfather was gathering up his umbrella and hat while addressing his grandchildren, "Right, shall we depart?" Who says "depart" to anyone?

During the summer, our Town Hall shows full length movies to the locals. Following the viewing of *The Help*, the MC expressed his concern for the vernacular used in the movie. He suggested the audience may require a volunteer interpreter, first to decipher the American slang, but secondly to understand the Southern Black dialect. I wisely did not raise my hand.

Getting through Customs at Heathrow Airport is always an adventure. Each year, the Customs Agent asks me for different information. The first year, as I was staying 6 months (the maximum stay for a visitor to the UK). I was asked to show that I did indeed have enough money to cover the duration of my visit. Luckily, I had a recent ATM slip that listed the current balance in my accounts. The following year, I responded to the query of my visit as I was writing a book and doing research. I used the 'book writing' angle for three years, until the agent responded, "Haven't you finished that book yet?" Do they put those responses in the computer? Or did he just make a lucky guess?

P
People of Purpose & Postal Perks

Parish Pandemonium

On my first Sunday of worship in my village, I chose the beautiful St. James' Parish Church. This lovely landmark is a monument to the prosperity of the wool trade at one time. Built approximately 500 years ago, it encompasses a perpendicular style tower "...with pinnacles topping the diagonal buttresses and a pierced parapet with ogee arches" (Simon Jenkins, "England's Thousand Best Churches"). To say it is a magnificent edifice is an understatement. Two reasons why I was attracted to St. James' were that it was only a "stone's throw" (no one really knows how far that is) from my holiday let and its historical relevance to the community. I am awakened each morning to the peal of its eight bells, filling the air with lovely music—almost like having God's alarm clock wake you.

I was moved by the words of Reverend Canon David Cook, who wrote a poignant Lenten message in the village paper that week, entitled "Listen to the Sounds of Silence". Vicar Cook wrote "for it is only when we are silent and undistracted from the noises of our frenetic world that we give ourselves a chance to hear the still, small voice of God, ... as quoted in the Psalms, 'Be still and know that I am God'". Those words appealed to me, as I am surrounded by more silence than I have ever experienced in a lifetime, except for possibly nine months in the womb. And in fact, God is speaking to me everywhere—the wind in the trees, the birds chirping their sonatas, the creaking of the timbers as the sun heats the house, the clicking of the radiators, the rain on the slate roof tiles, and even the sounds of footsteps on the cobblestones. On some days, the silence is deafening!

This particular Sunday was Mothering Sunday in England, which is a Christian festival, celebrated throughout Europe that falls on the fourth Sunday of Lent. Secularly it has become a celebration of motherhood in the UK, synonymous with Mother's Day celebrated by Hallmark in the US. The children of St. James' Parish School entertained the congregation with songs, written thank-you messages for their Mummies (of which brought all the women to tears), and handing out of flowers to each woman in attendance. It was positively blissful watching these small children traverse the sanctuary with yellow bundles of daffodils. Blissful, but noisy!

The pews are the original pews from who knows what century, when the people were shorter in stature. Consequently, the average gentleman today is unable to sit comfortably on the hard, cold, wooden benches, which creak with every movement. Due to Mothering Sunday, many families were in attendance, all of which included small children under the age of 2 years. There did not seem to be any 'cry room' available, so the charming noise of crying babies echoed throughout the "pinnacles topping the diagonal buttresses and pierced parapet" of the perpendicular tower. Glory, what a cacophony of sound accompanied the organ and congregational choral responses. The singing (and crying) went on and on for over an hour, including seven hymns, each with four or more verses, from their original hymnal. I found it was easier to sing the King's English dialect ("O, Lawd my Gawd! Whon awye un awesome won'da..."), than to speak it. Upon saying 'Good Morning' to my pew mates, the American accent was bothersome to the children sitting in front of me, and they kept turning around to see if I had two heads, or at least a very funny mouth. I'm sure their Mummy cautioned them to "not be afraid, the lady is from America".

Alas, the service was over and I had been musically fulfilled, but felt somewhat remiss in the Vicar's "talk" (verses "sermon"), mostly due to the poor amplification of the sound system as well as all the extraneous sounds. There was only one exit door, and it took another half-hour for everyone to greet the Vicar and the Curate upon exiting. Alas, it was my turn with Vicar Cook and I was able to share my delight in his article of Lenten "Silence" he had written and the apparent contradiction within today's service. We both got a 'chuckle' out of the inference.

Despite the hard pews, drafty apse, vocal babies, insufficient amplification, and lengthy hymns, there was delightful awe and wonder in God's house. I was able to see and hear God in the music, hushing of the mothers to their tired children, beauty of the daffodils waving within the children's arms, blessings of the mothers by their children, sunlight streaming through the stained glass, greetings of the friendly parishioners, warmth of the message, and the ever-comforting words of the scriptures and The Lord's Prayer. Amongst the pandemonium, there was an undercurrent that was welcoming and brought me home again.

St. James' Parish

"I like the silent church before the service begins, better than any preaching." ~ *Ralph Waldo Emerson*

Lollygagging in the 'Lane'

Behind one of the local village hotels is a tiny lane for pedestrian use. This lane runs right in front of my little cottage, so I get to see a great deal of the locals coming and going from the High Street. I find it more relaxing than watching television or listening to music, and more entertaining than reading a good book. I simply perch myself in my garden or at my front window and watch the foot traffic moving 'to and fro'. For my amusement, I make up stories of the people strolling by, observing their pace, company, attire, and anything that catches one's eye.

In the early morning, there are the Mums with strollers walking with their primary children up to the school. Smart looking kiddos in their uniforms, marching ahead of Mum and the stroller, so as not to be associated with the 'little one' crying in the pram. Younger siblings are ever so annoying!

By 8 AM, the women are walking at a brisk pace carrying their totes and headed for the Co-op, Fruit & Veg, Butcher, or Baker. And along the way, they will drop their letters in the red post box. Then they tote their carrier bags back home and start their daily chores. Later in the morning come their husbands, strolling, as they are in no particular hurry. They are getting their paper, then stopping for a cup of coffee and killing as much time as possible so as not to interfere with their wife's duties at home.

By 10:00, the wives have 'pegged' the laundry and they are headed to their church meetings, Zumba® classes, or meeting a friend for 'a cuppa' on the High Street. Later that morning, the husbands are headed back to their homes to smear a dab of dirt on their faces and sprinkle some water under their arms so as to look as though they had been 'working in the garden' in the wife's absence. The wife, being an understanding woman, goes along with this charade daily. After all, the houses are much to close together to have any disagreements that could be overheard and re-hashed along the 'Lane'.

After lunch, the tour bus drivers 'dump their load' in front of the Hotel, and send the little lemmings out for a walk. They stroll the High Street, and inevitably find their way to my little Lane to gawk at the quaint gardens, charming cottages, and wonder what 'interesting people' must reside in each abode. "Why, they must be so lucky to live here and be surrounded by all this beauty," they say. (How right they are!)

Later in the afternoon, the high school aged teens amble by on their way from buying their crisps and sweets at the Co-op or One Stop. They are in a hurry to get home and remove their wool uniforms and tights. Within the hour, they are back on the Lane showing a great deal of leg in their shorty shorts and thoroughly enjoying each other's fleshy company. Then caregivers from Mill House Residents Home appear to walk with their charges and their various types of equipment—"canes, frames, and wheel chairs...oh my".

In the early evening, along come the joggers, making all of us 'people watchers' most uncomfortable and feeling the guilt of watching vs. walking. Then the lovers appear, walking hand in hand, looking at each other starry-eyed, and not taking a bit of notice of the gardens. They only have 'eyes' for each other.

But of all the 'Lane' walkers, none are more priceless than the dog walkers. Every variety of dog known to man walks in our Lane, as well as some questionable breeds (dogs, not their owners). And each owner is smiling from ear to ear, as though it is a privilege to be accompanied by this veritable ball of fur. The only thing more enjoyable than walking one's dog is to meet another dog walker and let the canines have a 'good sniff' of each other.

As well, at any given time, the lane is full of pigeons, jackdaws, crows, and wrens. This is because my gardener puts out pounds of birdseed every morning at many of the cottages to keep them coming back. I'm surprised the Lane isn't entirely white-washed with bird poop!

This little Lane of mine is quite a gem and watching the traffic going by is an activity of which I never tire. After all, I am one of the lucky ones who live 'on the Lane'.

> *"I just want to go through Central Park and watch folks passing by. Spend the whole day watching people. I miss that."* ~ Barack Obama

Chatting with Ronnie

It is almost 10:00 AM! I was finishing a book last night and stayed up way past midnight. But that is no excuse. I hear the lawnmower coming through the gate; that means Ronnie is here to mow my tiny lawn and it only takes him 5 minutes from start to completion. I throw on some clothes, go bounding down the stairs, open the door, and check if I can make him a cup of tea. Ronnie only shows up every fortnight, and I don't wish to miss our chats over 'a cuppa'. It's the only time I can sit outside, watch the tourists and locals on the lane, and have a good laugh with someone equally as entertaining as myself! Yes, it's 10:15 AM and the tourists are already making their pilgrimage up the lane to take photos of anything standing still and video anything that moves! I shudder to think how many people in Asia have seen me in my garden through snapshots of their trip to the Cotswolds. There is not a flower that goes unturned in their eyes. And even better, they now have me and Ronnie in the background. I'm sure they have labeled us 'lucky owners of charming cottage', unbeknownst that we are the 'renter and her gardener'! But Ronnie and I get a chuckle out of it anyway. The waiters appear from the Hotel, which is just across the lane, carrying a load of rubbish to the bins. Ronnie and I put wagers on who will pick up the dropped debris on their way to the bins. We laugh when we both lose, as the waiters ignore the dropped bits and kick it to the side on their return.

Locals stroll up and down the lane on their way to the High Street for shopping. We make up stories about who they are and what they will buy and enjoy a good laugh at their expense. As they return, they make up stories about why the American lady has kidnapped the gardener and what she plans to do with him! Ronnie and I giggle at their fantasies.

A workman arrives next door to replace some glass in the new holiday let. He takes his level out of the van and goes to work. Ronnie says, "I wonder why he has a spirit level?" "What in the world did he call it—a 'spirit level'? "The spirits in the bubble", says he. Again, I laugh a little too loudly at the unusual name of a simple tool, Ronnie laughs at me laughing, and the workman shakes his head at both of us. I get such enjoyment out of the names of everyday objects over here.

Ronnie and I compare stories of growing up in a different world at a different time. A time when we went off to play and didn't return until after dark. The difference being, my mum would hold my dinner. Ronnie's mum warned him if he returned late, his plate would "go in the dog". As he returned to the dog licking a plate and asked if that was his dinner, his Mum only replied that "his brothers ate the meat off it, and the dog licked the rest". And now, Ronnie reports, his Mum watches telly (TV) and complains how the mothers of today treat their children. That gives us a good laugh as well. Ronnie declares his Mum is still alive. How young is this buck that I have corralled into my yard with a simple cup of tea? The answer is, "Who cares?". The man understands my humor and laughs at my jokes—he's a 'keeper' in my book.

Alas, he has finished his cup of tea ("a little milk, no sugar"), and is off to make another unattached woman happy for 30 minutes and a good mow job! 'Tis a bit sad, but one must find entertainment wherever and whenever she can! I can only pray for more rain and the grass to grow faster. Or maybe Ronnie would stay longer with a glass of wine!

"When I'm by myself, I'm not threatening at all. I get many more invitations than I would if I were traveling with anyone else, especially with a man. But I'm rarely alone. I sit on a park bench and I'm not alone because I pick a park bench where somebody interesting is sitting." ~ Rita Gelman

Did I See You in Church Today?

The longer I stay in this charming village, the more people I recognize from my past! I don't quite understand it, but it seems everyone I know has a twin in England, and more specifically in this place. Is it possible there are only a finite number of DNA molds, and after so many are produced, we start over again? I know it seems strange, but I have 'sightings' of 'people I have known' all over town.

One particular Sunday, I attended the local Methodist Church and later a concert at St. James' Parish. The concert was a visiting choir from a small town near Brighton, England. They sang beautifully, only to be enhanced by the magical acoustics within St. James'. As I looked from singer to singer, I recognized about five people from San Diego. Now, of course, they were not my California friends, but their similarities were so significant I had a few 'double takes'. How bizarre!

So, I have some time to think about this today. Is it merely the fact that I am missing my friends and, therefore, seeing resemblances that are not actually there? Or, is it possible that we do have one or more twin in other parts of the world. And, of course, there is also the possibility that during the past months I have actually forgotten what my US friends look like, and the similarities are only in my mind. Oh, I cannot possibly accept the last possibility. I am too young to be having those mind-altering episodes, surely.

It is a conundrum, and one I won't dwell on too long as I have much bigger things to think about. But suffice it to say, I have seen many of you walking the streets of my village, performing in concerts, or simply within the pews of a tiny little church in a tiny little village, in a tiny little country across the Atlantic. It should also be noted, that on my trip recently to Norway, I did not see one person I knew. Quite a different set of DNA molds there, some almost randomly assembled!

I have also noted that the women in my little village are rather plain next to American standards. Not necessarily ugly, just not quite all 'put together'. There is not a lot of extra money spent on make-up. Even the young girls have that 'fresh scrubbed' look and do not go out of their way to make themselves stand out. Maybe the American women do not want to look like anyone else in the world, so therefore artificially enhance that with which they were given.

Sensible clothing is on the average village woman—anything that they can put over a pair of black tights. Often the younger girls forget their skirts altogether and wear just the tights with a blouse. (Not exactly a trend-setting look!) What I don't quite understand is that there is a 'hefty' number of women within the "traditional women sizes", and yet the stores only sell up to size 18. Where do the larger women shop? Is there a Lane Bryant somewhere on the Backends (that's the street behind the High Street)? Are there 'Women's Catalogues' available at the News Agents? Or do they send after all their clothing from Amazon (which are made in China, of course!) It is a well-guarded secret, as I have tried to ask some of the traditionally-built women where to buy the "Queen" sized pantyhose. They just stare at me with one eyebrow cocked. I'm never quite sure if they don't want to tell me where they shop, for fear I will buy their clothing before they get there? Or is it possible, I have once again insulted the "Queen" by insinuating she is overweight? My guess is these questions will still be a mystery to me at the end of my stay and I will carry them with me unanswered back 'across the pond'.

> *"Your "look-alike" may be the result of one of the various possible futures happening simultaneously!"*
> ~ Vishwanath S J

Bird Man of Back Ends

One summer I stayed in a 2-bedroom cottage on the Back Ends. I could walk to either end of the High Street and connect with the Back Ends, or even more conveniently cut through at the side of Cotswold House Hotel. There was a delightful path that meandered along the side of the Hotel, past the Spa, and came out about a block from my cottage.

There were several perks about walking the short-cut. One, there was a small croquet park for Hotel guests with a few benches around the grassy area. Often, I would walk to this small park and take my spot on a bench just for the ambiance of the quiet, shady space. I often took a book or my crossword puzzle to fill the time. As well, this small park was a resting point on my way from shopping or following a bus outing.

After a quick break at the park, I would continue on my way to the Back Ends cottage. Along the way, I would often see Mr. Coop resting on his chair beside his bird feeders. Mr. Coop has spent all of his life in my village, and most of it living on the Back Ends. In his retirement years, he began making bird feeders which he sold for a ridiculous low price to anyone interested. Most of us who stopped had little interest in feeding the birds; it was to have a chat with this memorable gentleman who had lived so many years in the area. Oh, we always bought a bird feeder, because it was just our way of saying 'thank you' to Mr. Coop for chatting and imparting such colorful stories of days gone by.

It did not take too much imagination to picture Mr. Coop in his heyday. He frequently wore a jaunty cap that gave him a mischievous air. The hat alone could probably tell a few stories of its own. He loved holidays in Scotland which resulted in a new Tam-o-shanter every year. His cap was his trademark. At any rate, one could not pass this marvelous man without a good chin wag (and to purchase a bird feeder, of course).

"A bird does not sing because it has an answer. It sings because it has a song." ~ Chinese Proverb

Postal Perks: Packages from Home

My first trip overseas for an extended stay of six months was a learning experience. In my mind, utilizing the luggage for immediate needs and sending a box of summer clothing and extra cosmetics seemed like a 'jim-dandy' idea. And that is what I did. The box weighed 18 pounds but it wasn't too big, so I took it to the Postal Annex a day before I left home. The lady at the counter immediately warned me that UPS pricing was prohibitive and I should re-consider using U.S. Postal Service. She guaranteed delivery in 8 days. Well that didn't seem so bad, until she gave me the pricing of $141.46. Holy cow, I wasn't sure the items of clothing cost that much originally! But it was already boxed and my luggage was full to the brim, so I forked over the money without complaint. I was afraid to ask what UPS would charge.

Now I have sent packages from the UK many times and

know not to put down the full value, but for some reason that bit of information escaped me that day. When asked the value, I put down $250.00, just because I know the track record of the US Postal Service. What I forgot was the UK Customs charges, which were based on the estimated value of the package! Bad move on my part. As if the original cost of sending the package wasn't off putting enough, the saga continues.

For 30 days I tracked the package from the US to the UK. I knew it was somewhere in England, but the area was unknown. Didn't they say "8 days" at the Postal Annex? Possibly I misunderstood; maybe they said "8 weeks"? At any rate, at about day 30 I got a note from the Royal Mail Parcel Force. It listed the following duty charges: Customs Duty £15.77; Import VAT (value added tax) £46.96; and a Clearance Fee of £8. All in all, my Customs fee on my package due was £70.73, which translates to around $113.03. My little shipping folly cost me $254.49! What was I thinking? All that for three pairs of cut offs, a pair of slippers and sandals, four short sleeve shirts, some shampoo and hairspray and shower gel; a book and magazine, a gown and housecoat, and some crossword puzzles. The shipping actually cost more than the clothing and sundries total worth!

For the less experienced traveler, one might learn a lesson here (of course the more experienced traveler is already laughing hysterically). Even if I had paid an extra fee for heavier luggage, it would not have averaged $250.00. As well, in the past 30 days, I have passed a Crabtree and Evelyn shop where I get my shower gel and my brand of hair spray and shampoo is stocked at the village shops. Of course, it was suggested by several people that I should just consider buying whatever I could not pack, but I did not listen. You've got to love the wisdom you acquire in retrospect.

So, I have my very expensive summer clothing that I can only hope will get warm enough to even wear. In the meantime, I continue to wear my long pants, long sleeves, vest, wool socks, and occasionally two layers of shirts just in the house throughout April and May. As well, it is warmer outside than in the house. It seems that the Cotswold stone, albeit lovely, is not all that efficient at insulating. But not to worry, my box has arrived and I itemized each item that I sent to be worth about $20.00 each. I will layer them with pride and never look back on any possible mistake on my part. In the end, they will be donated to a Charity box before returning home. I have also vowed not to buy gifts for others. I won't be able to get anything extra in my luggage that is bigger than a bobby pin, which by the way, they continue to sell in the hardware store/post office in town. Who still wears bobby pins, for crying out loud?

"Dirty clothes weigh more. Wash before packing."
~ Marilyn Honea

"On a long journey even a straw weighs heavy."
~Spanish proverb

Q
Queue Quietly

Is There a Rule to Queue?

Queues are England's answer to keeping more than 2 people civilized whilst waiting. But I have yet to figure out the rules. It seems there are different rules for each circumstance.

This morning I was the third customer behind the outdoor ATM at the bank. In America, it is good practice and common sense not to get too close to those ahead of you and infringe on 'their space.' So, as I was waiting, I turned toward the opposite direction and was reading some of the signs in the store windows. When I turned back, I was now #5. How did that happen? It seems I left a little too much space between myself and #2. People just filled in the gap versus going to the end of the queue. I had to talk myself into calming down and convince myself I was in no hurry and just let it go (not my usual reaction to someone breaking into a queue!). I did, however, try to gain eye contact with the two people who cut in front of me, and would you believe, they would not even look in my direction?

There are always queues for the bus at the local bus stop. However, when the bus comes, everything goes awry. First of all, one must step aside to let the passengers off the bus first. Then the pensioners (OAPs) get on, as they don't pay and just show a pass, thereby snatching all the good seats. By this time, no one knows who was in line and it is all happenstance. If there are rules for the bus queues, it quite often escapes you by the time you are able to embark.

Then there are queues for taxi stands. When you are at the larger stations in London, there is quite a logistical arrangement with porters making sure everyone gets their appropriate turn. However, if you are in the villages, the taxi goes to whoever can run the fastest and zip in the back door. One needs to have a firm grip on the door handle or you can lose an arm if someone jumps in ahead of you.

Queuing up for the train is also hazardous. Your best bet is to go first class so that you can position yourself near the front of the train to get on. Most of the passengers hover around the middle of the train. But Brit Rail likes to mess with your head, and will occasionally put first class at the rear of the train just to see how fast you can run with luggage in the opposite direction. Once you are secure in first class and the first-class glass doors shut, you can smile at all the commoners who are crowded into the other cars and often standing between the cars. That satisfaction lasts quite a long way down the tracks.

When one is in the village, familiarity is the best method. If you can say the shop owners name or he/she says yours, you are automatically at the front of the queue. Therefore, it pays to learn your shop owners' names when you first get to town.

There is only one critical rule that all must abide: THE PENSIONER GOES FIRST! Do not try to change it, ignore it, or feign to not know it because you are new in town. It won't work. They know their rights. After all, they fought in WW2, or they know someone who went down on the Titanic, or they can recite the last 10 English Kings/Queens in order and years served. They have earned the right. They go first, get the best seats, and never stand longer than they can count. It is as it should be. Until you reach the stage of old age pensioner, you must give way and smile when you greet them. Otherwise, those canes pack a nasty wallop on the shin and the trolleys and frames (walkers) will run over your feet!

Queue, what queue?

"It's when the world comes to an end that you don't mind waiting your turn or if someone jumps the queue."
~ Anthony T. Hincks

The Quest for a Quiet Corner

The first summer I made the journey to the Cotswolds, I felt I owed it to my husband to 'take him along' on something I knew he would enjoy. After all, he did help me get there (his pension and life insurance). So, I boarded the Holland America Ryndam in Dover to see the scenic Fjords of Norway. The trip took seven days, and I was looking for a quiet corner to lose myself in for at least 6 of those days. After being in my quiet village, relaxing onboard ship was like seven days on Dover Hill during the Olimpick games—people everywhere.

The meals, the excursions, the casual conversations all blend in together until you are not sure of anything except what day of the week it is. That's because they daily 'change the day' written on the carpets in the elevators. I found a great deal of solace in my room, but I had to leave so they could clean at least two times per day. I also had a great little spot in the Ocean Bar, with my own private steward to keep my glass of wine filled. Those were my 'safe' places.

I remember Tuesday very well. It was the day we docked in Kristiansand and after my long day in Oslo, I declined leaving the ship. I had breakfast in my room and took a late shower around 10:00. While in the shower, I heard the alarm go off, the one with seven short blasts and a long blast, which means 'abandon ship'! As I am quickly drying off remembering I must "dress in warm clothing, take any medications, and proceed to Area Four on Deck Six for the lifeboats", the cruise director came back on the PA system to declare this was a "drill" for crew members only. My adrenaline was pumping now, so I decided to go in search of a new 'quiet corner'. As luck would have it, there was no one on Deck Six and all the lounge chairs were abandoned. What a treat! I settled myself mid deck where the breeze was delightful and proceeded to open a new novel. Five minutes into my meditative state, the alarm blasts sounded again, and all the crew descended on Deck Six wearing their yellow life preservers and surrounded my deck chair. All were chatting in their various languages, so it resembled an outdoor sanctuary with the congregation all speaking in tongues. I was locked in, nowhere to go, no way to get out, no exit in sight. Was this a conspiracy? It all lasted about 15 minutes, which seemed more like 45 minutes to me.

Looking back, the best reason to cruise was for a good

bed (mattresses in holiday rentals leave something to be desired). I would lay on my bed with hands and feet in each corner, looking like a model for Da Vinci. It was pure luxury, and I frequently spent time in my cabin until the next meal or glass of wine was imminent. At the end of the week, I looked forward to returning to my little 'cocoon' in the Cotswolds where life is quieter and slower paced. Mattresses, crowds, and liquor aside, the most difficult part of the cruise was going alone. That was the only time I have sailed alone. I do miss the carpets that told what day it was, however.

"In life, it's not where you go, it's who you travel with."
~ Charles M. Schulz

R
Raindrops on Rooftops

Raindrops Keep Falling on my Head...

My favorite sound to wake up to is the pitter-patter of raindrops. It's the trickling I wait for most of the year in California, typically in vain. After all, "it never rains in Southern California" ... ah, but that's another song for another time.

One particular morning, the pitter-patter kept lulling me from my drowsy state under my eider-filled duvet. This shelter protected me from all the elements—cold, nightmares, and all things that go bump into the night. I knew it was freezing still outside my down-filled haven, but I was drawn by the sound at my window. My feet recoiled as they touched the floorboards, which were even colder than I anticipated. I lifted the blackout shade, and there is a waterfall running down each pane. Rain, oh glorious rain. I used to read a story when I was young about Susan Samantha Cottonwood who was afraid to go out in the rain. Poor Susan, such a whiner! I would love to dance in the rain, pajamas and all. It always feels so clean and smells so wonderfully inviting. Although there was a hedge surrounding my garden, it was only four feet high, and the sight of an old woman dancing in her garden at seven o'clock a.m. was probably more than the neighbors needed to see. Then again, they are never surprised by what the Americans do anymore.

Instead, I made a pot of tea and looked for a good book on the shelf. Ah yes, here's a good one: Fifty Shades of Grey.

Hmm, it took a few pages before I realized it was not a book about the English weather! Maybe something a little less feverish was called for.

Outside, the music of pitter-patter continues, and I cannot take my eyes off the droplets as they cascade down the windowpanes. What a glorious sound and sight. It's worth waiting the six or seven months in California just to hear it again in the English countryside.

The flowers in the garden were standing at attention, drinking it all in, and literally blooming with delight. Although the birds were quiet and hiding under the hedges, they too seemed to be enjoying the water views, huddling together with awe. I knew it wouldn't last forever, but for a few hours I would enjoy the sights, sounds, and smells of the rain. Then, when it was finished, I would don my raincoat and walk in the aftermath, filling my nostrils with the floral scents, and splashing in a mud puddle or two. And in my head, I would be dancing in my garden, oblivious to my neighbors and pretending the world is all mine and I am the only one in it. Pitter-patter: it's a magical refrain.

A crown is merely a hat that lets the rain in.
~ Frederick the Great

Thy fate is the common fate of all; Into each life some rain must fall. ~ Henry Wadsworth Longfellow

The Rooftop Arms

One would think "The Rooftop Arms" referred to a lovely pub, small hotel, or B & B, but no—it is the name I assigned to my bedroom at the very top of the Rooftops House, where I took up residence my first summer in the UK. Upon first inspection at the series of circular stairs leading up to the second-floor bedroom, I took pity on my knees and decided the ground floor bedroom would be just right, but the owner insisted I climb the staircase to see the pinnacle piece de resistance. And it was well worth the climb! The lovely room had windows on three sides, each affording a marvelous view. Every rooftop within a radius of at least two hundred-seventy degrees was visible from this room. Every roofline, each individual chimney design, the sheep on the hills, and the moss on the roof shingles, were all framed within each windowpane. For once I was glad to have come at the end of winter, as I could look past the still-bare trees all the way to Dover's Hill on the other side of town. One could not ask for a more beautiful view of the village itself; it was a bit like looking down on a miniature display.

It was a vista one can't adequately describe with mere words, though it does remind me of this poem from Saint Gregory of Nyssa:

"In wintertime everything that is lovely withers away.
All the leaves, which are the natural crown of the beauty of the trees'

all from the branches and are mingled with earth.
The song of the birds is silent, the nightingale
flies away, the swallow sleeps and the
dove leaves its nest...."[1]

How delightful it will be, I thought, to observe the changing of the seasons from this lofty nest among the trees. In the past few days, Spring had indeed begun to show her face. Some budding was evident in the trees, crocuses were lifting their heads up from their winter sleep, and daffodils were starting to bloom. The dove had returned in his entire splendor, and Solomon's song of the impending season was playing everywhere:

"...'Arise, my darling, my beautiful one, come with
me. See!
The winter is past, the rains are over and gone.
Flowers appear on the earth; the season of
singing has come, and the cooing of doves is heard
again in our land.'" [2]

At night, I left all the shades up on my rooftop aerie so I could see the limbs of the trees swaying in the breeze. I remember as a child being frightened of the tree limbs hitting my window and the shadows passing back and forth around the room. But there is something incredibly soothing about this sight in my mature years. It reminds me of arms, gently hugging me. I picture myself embraced by the loving limbs and rocked gently to sleep, as in the arms of a loving mother. The wind in the trees became a nightly lullaby. I would be

---
1 The Holman Christian Standard Bible. (1999). Song of Songs 2:10-12.
2 Ibid.

lulled to sleep within the Rooftop Arms, oblivious to world anxieties and domestic concerns. Sheer and utter peace! And each morning as I woke, the arms of the trees released me to a new day with all the promise and anticipation of the impending Season. Soon, the leafy, embracing arms would shade my daily existence from any harm and provide my need for solace and tenderness when evening comes again. How wonderful to be so far away from home, and yet find such tranquility in a foreign place!

"The queen was settling on the edge of the bed, ungainly with hesitation and at the same time exquisite in her grace, like a heron landing in a treetop."
~ *Megan Whalen Turner*

"An oak tree and a rosebush grew,
Young and green together, Talking the talk of growing things-
Wind and water and weather.
And while the rosebush sweetly bloomed

The oak tree grew so high
That now it spoke of newer things-
Eagles, mountain peaks and sky.
"I guess you think you're pretty great,"
The rose was heard to cry,
Screaming as loud as it possibly could to the treetop in the sky.
"And now you have no time for flower talk,
Now that you've grown so tall."
"It's not so much that I've grown," said the tree, "It's just that you've stayed so small. "
~ Shel Silverstein

S
Sights, Sounds, and Scones

Skype Mum

Today marked a milestone for a loveable octogenarian: my mother used Skype for the first time. Danielle (her granddaughter) took her laptop when she went to see Mum at her retirement village in San Diego. They then skyped me in the UK so Mum could see my face and know that I am okay. Mind you, I had called her every week except one, and she had called me that week. But this was a thrill for her. She was so excited to see me that she kept forgetting to talk. She would run outside and catch people in the halls to invite them in to "come see my daughter in England." I felt like I was Mum's "Show and Tell" for the week.

What good fun it was to see her so enjoy modern technology. Well, it was the neatest thing since she learned how to use the cell phone (that's dialing, of course, not sending or receiving text messages; those had been taught and failed!). After several minutes of making small talk with many of Mum's neighbors, I tried in vain to get her to concentrate on a conversation with me. But it was just too overwhelming for her. She even insisted Danielle take the computer upstairs to the lobby and catch people coming out of the dining hall! Danielle, the good granddaughter that she is, headed upstairs with the computer, and all the while I was yelling at the top of my lungs, "Help me. I've been kidnapped and am stuck inside this stupid box. Can anyone get me out!" (Don't you just love embarrassing your kids!) Poor Danielle, just as she was about to pull the plug on me to get me to silence, we reached the lobby. Personal note: Don't ever let people carry you around while you are skyping (Is that a verb?). I instantly got motion sickness and made a mental note to purchase some Dramamine before the next call.

To say our communication was a success was an understatement. I knew Mum may never be happy with just a phone call again, and the experience was just as enjoyable to all her friends who participated. Well, this certainly put Mumsy a notch up on the popularity pole at the retirement village. Believe me, the popularity issue goes well into our golden years. One would hope that this one character flaw would be left behind in junior high, but alas, we can carry it with us right up until the discussion of "Who had the most flowers at their Memorial Service" or "My, my, such a few people showed to say goodbye at the funeral." This is not necessarily good news for all us Baby Boomers now entering the "senior" status. We were born to be popular. It makes one wonder as to the types of funerals that will make history as the Boomers are laid to rest.

But I digress from the excitement of the day, which was Mummy closing the timespan of eight hours just to see her daughter in England. That seems so minor for us who are used to technology, but to a woman eighty years young gaining eight hours is a definite landmark. You rock, Mum.

"I told him the computer was frozen and he tried to unfreeze it with a blow dryer." ~ unknown

The Sounds of the Village

One can almost tell the time by the distinguishing sounds within the village. At 2:00 a.m. there is the soft sound of gravel crunching, followed by the tinkling of bottles when the milkman delivers the milk to the stoop. At 6:00 a.m. the roosters on the farm on the Back Ends begin their wake-up serenade. Between 7:00 and 8:00 the doves start their cooing and the pigeons try out their alarm-like "who-who-whooing." The bells of St. James Parish begin tolling the hour at 8:00 a.m. as well. One does not even bother staying in bed past 8:00, for the cacophony of outdoor "music" will rouse the soundest of sleepers. From 9:00 a.m. the gravel again crunches with people leaving for work, duffers heading out to the golf courses, and children traipsing off to school.

Between 10:30 and noon, the mailman enters the lane

and begins his rounds. The crunch of the gravel is subtler, as he pushes his bicycle and delivers his parcels, letters, and advertisements to each door. The stores in the village open around 10:00 and the women are pacing up and down High Street ducking into the various shops and filling their baskets or trolleys. The traffic on High Street also begins a steady flow through town, with the occasional "honk" at the lorry blocking the street or the pensioner crossing the street, unaware of traffic.

Throughout the morning, the peace is interrupted frequently by the drip, drop of rain sprinkling on the slate tile roofs and dripping from the eaves. Occasional gusts of wind transport the loose branch across the patio stones or rustle the leaves, just to let you know Mother Nature is alive and well.

In the afternoon, the sounds of children's laughter permeate the village. School's been dismissed for the day. Each household and teashop is alive again with the tinkle of spoons in cups as afternoon tea commences. This is my favorite of all the sounds and is not to be ignored. As everyone settles down for a cuppa you can hear the bleating of rams, ewes, and lambs from the nearby farms as they discuss the price of wool and when to shed their coats. The afternoon horse ride by the young girls in town is evident in the clip-clop of the hooves upon the pavement.

Around 6:00 the pubs begin filling with patrons and the obvious clinking of glasses can be heard. Everyone is greeted as a long-lost friend and toasts are made to good health as the foam settles on glasses of lager and pills. It's a happy time, evident in the laughter surrounding each establishment. The pubs are strategically located throughout the village, just far enough apart so you could be ejected from one and still be able to stagger on to the next. As sunset approaches, the jackdaw blackbirds begin their screeching from tree to tree, obviously envious of the libation they are being denied from the public houses.

Early dusk is always a cue for the rain to again present itself, partly to sober up the staggering crowd emerging from the pubs and to quicken the pace home to ready for the evening meal. Around 8:00 the clinking of cutlery upon china rings out from the restaurants and abodes within the village, as everyone enjoys the "dinner hour" and an ending to the day.

Each of these sounds, distinct and timely, is obvious to the average listener in tune with the life of the village. They are familiar and calming sounds that can pass by unnoticed, if one does not rely on their sense of hearing. Close your eyes, and listen to the heartbeat of the village.

Much silence makes a powerful noise." ~ African Proverb

A Scone Delight

It was raining, again. Not that I minded the rain, but it did restrict one's coming and goings. I had bought stamps at the post office and they lost their stick 'em in the dampness and had to be glued onto the envelope. The pages started to curl on my library book. My hair either had that "just washed" look or "hat head" from my raincoat hood. But there is one thing you can depend on when it rains in England—tea is always close at hand.

Although you can drink tea anytime, it is particularly delectable when it is raining. It is really the only thing that can take the chill off you. So, you let down your umbrella, enter the cozy tea shop, and a new sensation is awakened to make up for the damp day. Firstly, there is a lovely fire going in the fireplace that you can snuggle up to and warm your feet on the hearth. Although the woody smell of the fireplace tantalizes your nose, you begin to notice another aroma wafting throughout the room. What is that fragrance? It's the bouquet from heaven, surely. The waitress approaches and you order your tea and then she offers those magical words: "I have fresh scones, warm from the aga." Is there nothing that can please you more than that delicious phrase?

You decide on the warm scone, lest you disappoint the baker. You sip your hot tea in anticipation of the melt-in-your-mouth delicacy that is to come. And then the lovely biscuit arrives, about the size of Mt. Etna, to delight your growling tummy. You slowly split the buttery mountain and let the steam rise up and meet your nose, carrying the scent of butter, sugar, and raisins to your sinuses, clearing them to receive the marvelous aroma you have been eagerly awaiting.

But what is this? They have also included a small dish of Devon cream that melts instantly as you spread it on the warm scone. How delightfully sinful! And there is more—a dollop of strawberry jam, resplendent with whole berries, to place just on top of the cream. You take your time making sure the entire scone has been covered with the cream and jam, catching glimpses of other customers licking their lips in anticipation of your first bite. Slowly you raise the scone to your mouth, as you imagine your taste buds applauding the premier event. You take a bite. Pure ecstasy. You look around the room and smile at the other diners, letting them know it was worth the wait, and they let out a collective sigh for your supreme effort. Then it becomes a careful ballet of movements between a nibble of the scone extraordinaire and sipping the delicious blend of hot tea. The meeting of warm scone and cool cream, then washed with a steaming sip of specially blended tea leaves, is magical. The tongue tingles while accepting the juxtaposition of sweet and then bitter, combining in the perfect harmony of flavors.

Suddenly the rain has lifted and you are free once again to stroll down the lane, brilliant with all the colors of spring, awakening your other senses. Everything seems so much clearer now and you walk in the knowledge that life, as you know it, is perfect.

"More and more clearly as the scones disappeared into his interior he saw that what the sensible man wanted was a wife and a home with scones like these always at his disposal." ~ P.G. Wodehouse

"My mum refers to female genitalia as scones."
~ Leah Marie Brown

T
Travel, Tea, and Tubs

Cruising Solo

My husband loved to cruise. He loved the open sea, which is why he joined the Navy during the Korean Conflict, but from what he told me he never really sailed on any ships. Instead, he worked in supply at a Naval Air Force Base. When it came to vacations, he definitely thought cruise ships were the way to go. He loved getting to know the crew, meeting fellow Navy buddies in the bar, and generally being waited upon hand and food (oops, I meant foot). Yes, the unlimited food onboard a cruise ship was also appealing to him. It was the one time I could get him to dress for dinner without complaint.

We cruised together for many years—from the time when he could walk aboard on his own, to using a cane, then a wheelchair, and finally him driving a motorized cart aboard. Our last cruise together was ten months before he passed away. His dream was to die at sea and then be stored in the meat locker until reaching our destination. How I was supposed to manage both sets of luggage and a coffin remains a mystery.

I, however, am easily afflicted with motion sickness and really can't even look at the waves without fighting bouts of nausea. I once got "seasick" while looking in a fish tank! Hence, no aquariums were allowed in our house. But as my husband's health declined, we discontinued the tours of Europe that we had once enjoyed and turned to cruising so that we could continue to enjoy traveling together. I was always sleepy from the medication, and frequently loopy when mixing alcohol and Dramamine, but hubby did not seem to mind.

Though I had often expressed gratitude for my husband's support in my long-term stay in the Cotswolds, I felt I needed to do something just for him—a post-mortem thanks for his part in getting me to my destination. Hence the aforementioned seven-day cruise from Dover to the Fjords of Norway during the month of June. In truth, after three months on a foldout couch a week in a comfortable bed sounded like heaven to me. So, I obtained the necessary amount of motion sickness drugs and set off to Dover.

What I did not bank on was the memories we had shared cruising and how difficult it would be to experience them solo. In fact, the ship I sailed on, the Ryndam, was one we had sailed on before. I went through the motions of sharing a table with other diners, having a drink in the bar and making conversation with perfect strangers, going ashore to visit sites on my own, making it all look easy to those unaware. But it was hard; another one of the many "tough love" encounters I had endured during my years of widowhood. But we persevere, we survive, we grow stronger, and this too becomes easier over time.

There were some definite awkward moments by curious well-meaning observers. My comments included, "I'm dining alone tonight." This left them thinking there was still someone in my room who was unable to join me at that time. We must prevaricate at times to save face. Here is my advice to the solo travelers of the world: find another form of vacation entertainment. Cruising solo is restrictive. Guidance from my children when I told them my plans was to (1) drink more wine, and (2) learn to dance. I won't tell you which I chose as I don't specifically remember. Maybe I danced, maybe I didn't.

"He who is outside his door has the hardest part of his journey behind him." ~ Dutch Proverb

"I wasn't planning to lead, I was standing in the back and then everyone turned around." ~ Avery Hieber

Anchors Away!

My cruise to the Fjords was not just a thank you to my husband, or a respite for my paining back. I had decided to take a break from the simple life and dip my toe back into society before having to go back to my busy existence in America. After those quiet months in my village, however, it was more like diving in head-first.

The Captain of the ship was Dutch and somewhat difficult

to understand when he would make announcements on the PA system. With his broken English and even worse Norwegian quips, he was a delightful break from the Cruise Director. Did you know any future cruise directors in high school? He was the only male member of the cheer squad; or was the campaign manager for the most popular male/female running for class president; or he worked in the office for his elective hour shining this nose on the principal. You may not remember his name, but you do remember how annoying he was! (I don't mean to be gender specific here, but to date I have never been on a cruise with a female cruise director.) At any rate, enjoying one's own voice, being constantly "upbeat," and keeper of the most boring jokes in the world are definite prerequisites for the job.

On the fifth night into the cruise, as we were leaving Ulvik, the Captain told us of the sites we would see just after departure. Pulpit Rock and the longest suspension bridge being built in Norway definitely sounded like photo ops. Having acquired those pictures, I then went to the dining room for steak and lobster night. On my way to the dining room, there was a nasty sound coming from the bowels of the ship. About fifteen minutes later, the Captain came on the PA system to admit to a "problem." It seems someone forgot to lock the anchor in place (I wonder if that poor schmuck will ever crew again), and it had continued to feed itself out until it brought the ship to a standstill. Now, you don't just wench up the anchor on one of those big boys. You must reposition the ship until it is directly above the anchor so there is no drag, and then slowly bring it up. This means that the ship will continue to float about for some time, until the drag is reduced and all of the remaining anchor and chain have been brought back home. Well, you guessed it; all during dinner I stared at that stupid rock and suspension bridge that I had so hurriedly photographed earlier. It took about two hours for the whole process to be completed and the poor Captain had to eat crow while I dined on steak and lobster. Now I ask you, where was that glib cruise director when the Captain needed him? Nowhere near the bridge, I am sure. As luck would have it, however, we continued to listen to all the rhetoric the little twit could muster for two more days.

"The cure for anything is saltwater: sweat, tears, or the sea." ~ Isak Dinesen

A Trip on the MTA

The Kingston Trio recorded one of my favorite songs in 1959. It was a story of "Charlie," a man in Boston who got on the subway (MTA) and did not know the fare had increased in price. He was later unable to disembark due to "insufficient funds." I remember him as "the man who never returned." Well, this "extended travel" happened to me, once on the train and once on the bus. Most embarrassing—though it was not due to insufficient funds but rather to "traveler error". I cannot go further with my story without a disclaimer that I was traveling with other people and easily distracted. I won't go so far as to name them as the reason I was on the "MTA." It could just as easily have been my fault (but wasn't).

On the train to Torquay, we were to disembark at Norton Abbot. Unfortunately, we were close to the train door, but unable to get the door open. I don't know if you have ever ridden the trains in the UK, but opening the doors on the trains are often as complicated as turning on some of the showers in the B&Bs. On the older trains, you lower the window, reach on the outside of the door and turn the handle. Not something the average American traveler would be able to figure out in the eight nanoseconds they give you to disembark with your luggage. On the newer trains, the door will open at the push of a button; however, they hide the button! At any rate, we were unable to open the door. Before the purser got to us, the doors had automatically locked. He was very apologetic for our inconvenience (it's the British way), and wrote us a pass for the next station to reverse our way back to Norton Abbot. So very civilized. Were we charged extra for our mistake? Not a pence! Just apologies from the porter as if it was his fault.

The other error in judgment was taking the bus from Stow in the Wold to Moreton on Marsh. Unfortunately, someone in the group misread the bus destination, and before we knew it, we were on our way to Cheltenham, which is in the opposite direction. The light bulb didn't go off in my head until we reached the next station of Bourton on the Water. We quietly enjoyed the ride, as we were too embarrassed to admit our mistake. Later, the driver reminded us that we were at the end of the line in Cheltenham. At this point we had to confess our error and he laughed and took us back on the next route to Stow. This was another free ride for the Americans.

Now, the upside of these mistakes was that we got to see a bit of the countryside that we would have otherwise missed, and for no extra charge. The British Rail system and Pulham Coaches were gracious enough to overlook our brief faux pas. Of course, it gave them fodder for telling another "dumb American" story. On the other hand, these mistakes cost a bit of time and angst as to whether we might be reliving "Charlie's fate" in Boston. It should be mentioned that both of these mistakes were in the company of the same American visitors. No, I am not casting blame, just stating facts. They know who they are!

> *"Your grandma always had a terrible sense of direction. She could get lost on an escalator."*
> *~ Fredrik Backman*

> *"It's okay to get lost every once in a while, sometimes getting lost is how we find ourselves."*
> *~ Robert Tew*

Night Travels

I take the night flight when I leave San Diego and arrive about 3:00 p.m. in London town. I have eaten the last of my trail mix on the plane and will be eliminating peanuts for the next three weeks. Yes, I did have airplane food, but I was hoping for normal fare. Lukewarm curdled pasta for dinner and a frozen croissant for breakfast—yum! Do they store the food out on the wing during flight?

Two of my summers I had flown first-class, thanks to my American Airline miles. I enjoyed being one of the Pod People who dined with real silver, drank copious glasses of champagne, and then slept in a bed for the duration of the flight. The rest of six summers, however, my miles were gone and the party, so to speak, was over. I paid for a "World Class" seat behind Business Class, where there are only two seats on the sides with some extra legroom and a semi-recliner seat. The worst part of where I am sitting is that you can still see the first-class passengers. They're snuggling into their little pods like so many peas, pulling up their insular membranes, giving them the illusion of privacy, and preparing to be pampered for eleven hours. Then the unforgivable happens for us onlookers—they close the drape and you can no longer see how the other half lives. (That used to be me on the "other side"; now I know how Betty Broderick felt (a San Diego joke.) Thankfully I was able to buckle the existing seatbelt, without having to ask for one of those inconvenient extensions the flight attendant always forgets to bring you after she is uses it for demo purposes in the pre-flight instructions. On the other hand, it was most disconcerting to finally wedge myself into the seat, only to find out that all the controls from lighting to seat adjustments are on the insides of the chair and inaccessible! (This is beginning to sound like the Perils of Pauline!)[1]

Upon landing, customs went well, for a change. When asked if I was visiting friends or relatives in the Cotswolds for five months, I responded, "Friends." Then the agent asked me to name them—ha! After an eleven-hour flight, I couldn't remember my own name, much less those in my village. Finally, Lady Jean popped into my mind—always good to drop a "Lady" as an acquaintance. After emerging into the lovely London mist, I was shocked when there was no queue for the taxi. Little did I know that they had imposed a minimum taxi fee of £35 to

---

1 Marshall, George. (1947). *The Perils of Pauline*. Paramount Pictures.

my hotel three miles away. I'm not rich, but not stupid either.

My destination at the Hilton takes about three minutes as the crow flies; however, it always seems longer after eight consecutive roundabouts, designed to disorient you on exactly how far you have driven and which direction you are going. (London must look like a giant labyrinth in an aerial view with all their circles.) The hotel was pure luxury, however—crisp white Egyptian cotton sheets with a fluffy duvet to snuggle up into after a long, hot shower. It would be the perfect bed to sleep naked in, if it weren't for the fact that they never have a top sheet. I have always questioned if hotel staff take time to change the duvet cover between guests? I was asleep after half a crossword puzzle and one episode of Detective Vera, only to awake solidly at 3:00 a.m. and commence to writing this musing in order to kill time until the breakfast buffet opens. So began another summer adventure in the Cotswolds. My friend, Barry (whose name I totally forgot when speaking with the Customs agent) wouldn't be picking me up for another few hours, so I was presented with a choice: eat very, very slowly, or continue my healthy start on the book I keep giving Customs as a reason for my visit in the UK. At any rate, it was, "Goodbye, USA," and "Hello, UK" for another glorious stay. Eat your heart out, my US friends—I can't remember your names either!

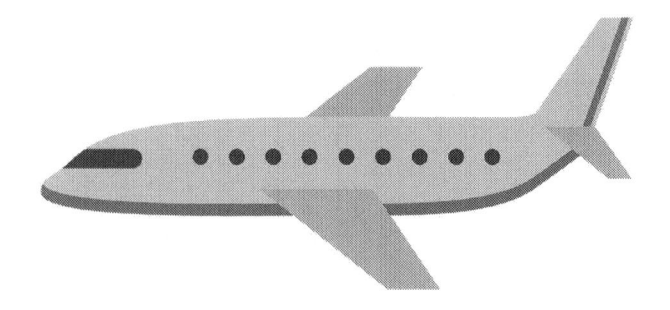

"All I really want to do is spend my life travelling the world, reading books that take my breath away, drinking all kinds of tea and occasionally write something. I mean is that too much to ask for?" ~ Unknown

Tiptoe to the Tea Shoppes

I am incredibly lucky to have several tea and coffee shops in my village. The best part about inclement weather is that you are never too far away from a port in the storm. One day, as I strolled from the library, I could see another dark cloud over my head that looked threatening. At that moment, I was between two teashops. (How civilized!) My only choices were to go forward or backward. A "local" does not make a run for it or deal with the nasty umbrella to ward off the impending storm. If you have any class at all, you merely stroll into the nearest teashop and wait out the waterworks. Timing is of the essence. The villagers know precisely when to enter the shoppe (just before the first drops fall), and how long to sip tea for the duration of the storm. In other words, is it a one-pot or two-pot rainfall? Of course, you can always supplement your pot of English blend with something sweet. A scone with clotted cream and jam will last about twenty to thirty minutes if you are also enjoying a conversation. If alone, you can extend your pleasure by working a crossword puzzle or reading a book. If you choose a piece of English sponge cake, it typically lasts for fifteen minutes. There is always the lovely piece of shortbread, which can last forever, unless you choose to dunk it, which is NEVER done by the locals.

So, there you have it, a continuous cycle. The clouds form, you make your casual entrance into the tea shoppe while there is still a table available, you assess the length of the downpour and order your tea and accompaniment accordingly. If you are a true Brit, you emerge from the teashop just as the sun has come out and you never have to open your umbrella. In fact, I am convinced that none of the locals are able to open their "brollies" at all, as they have rusted shut! And yet they carry them, without fail. Is it part of their dress code? Or are they born with one attached to their body, as third appendage? It is not known.

As the rain disappears, out the locals emerge from the shoppes, filling the sidewalks. That is also why they wear such clean raincoats; they never get wet. The only ones looking wet and bedraggled are the tourists who are too stupid to get in out of the rain before all the tables fill up in the tea shoppes.

What I haven't figured out is how they can drink all that tea and time themselves just right to get home before using the facilities. Even more puzzling, how do they maintain their weight with all those scones, shortbreads, cakes, et cetera? Again, these things are not known. Meantime, it is my mission to visit as many teashops as I can, come rain or shine.

"There are few hours in life more agreeable than the hour dedicated to the ceremony known as afternoon tea." ~ Henry James

Turtle in the Tub

On my second six-month sojourn, I decided to bring Mum along so she could experience the "thrills" the charming Cotswold villages have to offer. Because Mum required a wheelchair in Heathrow we had to go through the "Special Needs" line at Customs, which could be a bit tricky. There were several of us in an airport electric vehicle which seemed to zoom from the aircraft, through the catacombs of Heathrow airport, and finally back to the Customs area. We were in good shape, only one cart ahead of us. (Note to traveler: If requiring the Special Needs Customs line be sure to follow a cart of Americans or Canadians, for expeditious service.) Unfortunately for us, the cart in front was a group from Nairobi. They all needed to be fingerprinted, then checked, only to encounter severe delays if one of the prints comes up "questionable." After thirty minutes, we finally had our turn. The agent was not concerned with the two senior citizens or one ailing South African woman in our vehicle. I was the only one questioned, due to my truthful response to staying another six months. Fortunately, I happened upon the magic retort to the proverbial inquiry, "Why are you staying so long in the countryside?" It seems being a "writer" is the acceptable response of the day! They weren't interested in my finances, as they were last time I stayed. Presumably, "authors" are not expected to have money—only talent. (Note to reader: Talent also remains to be seen!)

After collecting our baggage, we were met by good friends, Barry and wife, for our road trip to the village. The three of us chatted about what had occurred in the past six months: updates on families, which village citizen had expired, what businesses had come and gone, and where to get the best fish and chips this month. Mum nodded off peacefully in the front seat, missing a lot of the points of interest pointed out by the three locals. I, however, was "home again," and loving it.

Our little rental cottage was a delightful site as we cruised into the village. We took a quick tour around, and then walked to the local hotel for dinner. I enjoyed my first half pint of Guinness in six months—why does the first glass always taste so good?

Mum had her mind on that lovely tub she saw in our cottage, and was anxious to return for a good soak. We stopped at the Co-op for some bath bubbles, and she excitedly immersed herself into the warm waters to soothe her aching body from the long flight, two-hour car trip, and one-hour dinner. All seemed right with the world.

And then it happened. Time to emerge from the tub. She let out all the water and proceeded to twist and turn, flex and extend, bend and rotate, all in effort to get out of the tub. But it was all in vain. She seemed permanently ensconced in her porcelain sarcophagus. Would she enjoy her three weeks in the village within the cottage tub? Oh, what to do? I tried lifting her, but her tiny body was now water-soaked and she seemed to weigh three hundred pounds! I took to the streets in search of a phone to dial 999 (The English version of 911). I located a delightful couple across the lane in the Rosetree cottage, who were vacationing from Holland. Although they did not know how to help me, they did let me use their mobile phone to call for assistance. The operator inquired as to my needs but could only offer one of three options: police, fire brigade, or ambulance. "Mother stuck in the tub" was not an option. I went back and proposed a plan to Mum regarding notifying the "ambulance, with strong attendants," which she immediately nixed. Plan B was to call my friend Barry, who was a retired fireman. Mother knew Barry from the road trip from Heathrow, and was not keen on seeing him again in her current state of undress. It was one thing to have her own daughter see her attempting to don her pajamas while stuck in a tub, but the thought of greeting visitors in her birthday suit was too much to bear. The next hurdle was back across the lane to direct a Dutchman in using a mobile phone out of his country. Does one use an international country code to access a private phone number in the village? It was all so confusing. We were never successful in completing the dialing hurdle of using a Dutch mobile in the English countryside.

Then it was back to the cottage tub to discuss Plan C: sheer determination. Well, that plan was a winner. Suddenly Mum was able to propel her legs over the edge and my adrenaline-pumped muscles were able to pull her forward, up, and out without incident. Mum and I have had wonderful laughs and adventures in my lifetime, but none so dramatic as trying to right a turtle on her back while lying in a tub. And to think I was worried about entertaining my lovely mum for three weeks. She provided more entertainment in an hour than I could ever have ever planned. The three-week adventure began with tension, fear, and anxious moments, and happily turned into gales of laughter. My only regret is not getting a picture to capture the fun for all of eternity.

"Planes, canes, and automobiles—connecting with your aging parents through travel." ~ *Valerie M. Grubb*

"Sometimes you will never know the value of a moment until it becomes memory." ~ *Dr. Seuss*

U
Unexpected

First Class Service

As mentioned, there is no greater luxury on the planet than to be one of the Pod People in first class, each snuggled in their own bed to sleep away the eleven-hour flight. You are being waited upon from before takeoff until just before landing at your destination. You start the flight with the lovely, warm wet towel to refresh yourself and whisk away the airport germs. Those towel treats continue off and on throughout the flight. Then comes the warmed, salted nuts and the first of many G&Ts of your journey. Then the dinner arrives after a linen placemat is placed upon the tray table. The food is a few steps above that food served to the steerage, along with poured wine (versus those miniature bottles that contain the years of poor grape production). No plastic ware in first class; only silver.

After dinner, the stewards help you lower your seats into horizontal position for a bed, bring you a pillow, blanket, and eye mask and tuck you in for the night. They will gently awake you for the morning breakfast with the aroma of fresh coffee and warmed croissants. It's a bit like flying in a four-star hotel.

The year my mother accompanied me, I decided she deserved to experience this treat at least once in her lifetime. She was not nearly as impressed as I was by the event, but then it takes a lot to impress "women of a certain age." She was a bit claustrophobic in the pod seats, simply due to the lack of privacy before the pod screens were raised. Shortly into the flight, she started rubbing her elbow. The male steward was at her side immediately, asking if he could make her more comfortable. Well, that was all it took to get her attention and she milked it for the rest of the trip. There was a constant stream of items being brought to and fro from the galley to make her journey more enjoyable—pillows, hot water bottles, wine, blankets, as well as frequent seat adjustments and assists up/down to the facilities. I'm quite sure British Airways is the only airline that stocks hot water bottles! If you ever want to impress your mother, invest in first class tickets to anywhere. I am grateful to my family for helping pay the way for this investment.

During her stay Mum and I traveled to Paris as well. Those three weeks gave her enough bragging rights with her senior friends for years to come.

"And in the end, it's not the years in your life that count. It's the life in your years." ~ Abraham Lincoln

Silver Will Tarnish

Friends in the USA continually ask me if I am growing tired of my beautiful surroundings in the English Cotswolds. I suspect they are more envious of my being in the most charming place on earth than worrying over my creature comforts. However, my response to their queries is that "silver will tarnish."

There are days when the weather is abysmal; of that there is no doubt. During my first weeks in April, I experienced infrequent sunshine and clear days, wind storms that would blow you off the sidewalk, torrential rains, freak hail storms, temperatures below six degrees Celsius, and even snow. When you see the sunshine, you grab your keys and abandon the house. You go for a nice long walk to window shop on High Street, take off on a blissful stroll through the pastures filled with wildflowers and newborn lambs, or hop on a bus and visit a neighboring village filled with new and different treasures to admire.

The rain is as much a fact of life in England as the sunshine is in California; however, one need only feast her eyes on the lush green of the hills and dales, admire the lovely flowering gardens, or smell the clean refreshing air following a rainfall to understand God's plan. That is when you appreciate the sensual delights of perpetual precipitation. It also allows time for slowing one's pace, enticing a good read, or enjoying an afternoon "lie-down."

The winds blow across the countryside, clearing the air and allowing Mother Nature the ability to transplant a multitude of delightful spores to germinate in a new home. The occasional change in wind direction brings new scents across the meadows of blooming "rape" (the English form of goldenrod), various excrement perfumes from the stables and farms, and the aroma of fish and chips from the neighboring kitchens. Yes, it is challenging when the wind and rain blow to keep one's feet on the sidewalk while carrying an umbrella. How else do you think they came up with the idea of Mary Poppins?

It is difficult for a California girl to deal with both dampness and cold; but that's why the Englishman placed a pub or a tea shoppe every five meters. It is truly delicious to be nursing a cuppa or sippin' a pint while cuddled around a roaring fire and sharing a spirited conversation with new friends.

So, rather than go into detail describing my delights and occasional setbacks of my new life to US friends and family, I resort to the phraseology of "silver will tarnish," hoping all will understand the analogy. An optimal style of living is much like a fine piece of silver; sometimes it is bright and shiny, sometimes tarnished, but always functional and durable, with the feel and taste of richness.

"Every cloud has a silver lining." ~ unknown

"If you change the way you look at things, the things you look at change." ~ Dr. Wayne Dyer

Sylvie, The Silver Spoon

The first time I saw her, she was standing amongst a pile of debris—boxes of china, glasses, cutlery, pots and pans, and various sundry of household items. She looked as disheveled as her surroundings. She wore a long pink nightshirt outlining her braless form, slippers on her feet (one black and one brown), curlers in her hair, and interestingly enough, nylons and a spectacular gold necklace the size of a bicycle chain. One could not tell if she was in a state of coming or going, that which was coming from bed or in the process of going out! She stood only about four-feet eight inches tall, but one could tell she could be a giant when need be. She apologized profusely for her state of undress, the condition of the apartment around her, and for the general state of affairs of the day. She had been up since early morning, preparing for me to take up residence in the house upstairs. She surely must have leapt out of bed at 5:00 a.m. and started cleaning. But the anxiousness she exhibited was not from meeting a new tenant, her state of undress, or the exhaustion of working since early morn. It was due to the fact that she had locked herself out of the upstairs, thereby unable to admit me into my new abode I had leased for the next six weeks. Instead, she was forced to greet me in the midst of a renovation project in the studio unit at the back of the house.

Of course, I could have turned my head and volunteered to wait in the front garden, but it was cold and damp and I needed to relieve myself of the morning tea that had accumulated in my bladder on the two-hour hire car ride from London. She graciously pointed me into a bathroom the size of an English phone box. In straddling the toilet, it was necessary to avoid a misplaced floor lamp, various clothing strewn about the postage stamp-sized floor, while bumping my knees on the wash basin. It's not that I minded the discomfort of the facilities, or the disarray in which I found my surroundings; however, I was concerned that I would be inhabiting this disorganized space in another six weeks when new renters were scheduled to occupy the upstairs unit. The upstairs and downstairs maisonette was to be my home for the next six months! Sylvie once again apologized for the state of the surroundings and explained they were in the process of renovating the downstairs studio before I was scheduled to move in. The plan, of course, was for her to be dressed and greeting me at the front door of the newly furnished and cleaned upstairs apartment and for me never to see the small studio until the renovations were completed. Ah, but that was before she had locked herself out of the front door of the main house. Sylvie was spinning around like a chicken in a cage trying to locate a set of keys amongst the debris.

Here was my first test as an American in a new land, to make the most of the situation with grace and dignity, thereby putting the distraught Silvie at ease. To that end, of course, I failed miserably. I fell into spasms of laughter, holding my sides and feeling the tears forming in the corners of my eyes. Sylvie likewise reacted with the same hysteria, and the thin veneer was broken and the bond of friendship began.

Sylvie forgot about her state of undress, ran to the neighbors to retrieve an extra set of keys, and proceeded to show me around her spectacular home with such pride and grace that one forgot all about her appearance and embraced the infectious demeanor of this beautiful lady. She was so proud of her former domicile and delighted that I would be inhabiting it during my time in the Cotswolds. The old-world furnishings mixed with modern conveniences—including an automatic clothes washer and dishwasher, a sparkling bathroom, and new linens—added to the general coziness of the abode. I was delighted and overwhelmed at my good fortune in "letting" an establishment over the internet sight unseen. I was equally mesmerized by Sylvie's warmth and charm.

It wasn't until several hours later that she arrived again at my front door, dressed in designer clothes, her hair perfectly styled, with eye-catching accessories, and the deportment of a classic "lady." Sylvie was transformed with all the beauty and quality of a polished piece of sterling silver. This magnificent lady proceeded to make me a dinner fit for royalty, including a rack of lamb, vegetables, the perfect glass of French wine, and a delicious strudel for dessert. We spent hours over dinner preparation and ultimate dining pleasure discussing all we had in common and making plans to deepen our new friendship during my stay. How wonderful to be greeted on my first day in my lovely village by the delightful and witty Silvie. She was initially like enjoying a picnic with plastic cutlery, transforming into an elegant dinner party with fine china and gleaming silver flatware.

"When you are not fed love on a silver spoon, you learn to lick it off knives." ~ Kajal Saxena

V
Visions

The Big Dipper

The English weather at night is just as unpredictable as it is during the day, which meant I never knew whether the treetop-level view from my first abode would be cloudy and overcast or filled with stars. Again, any view I had at this point was due to the stark branches of winter just before the trees bud in spring. I had not experienced summer from my rooftop sanctuary and was not quite sure how much visibility I would have once the trees were in full bloom.

One particularly glorious night the window show was a starry sky against the black backdrop of night. Right over my head was the Big Dipper, and it actually looked like the ladle was about to pour out some substance right onto my head. How delightful to drift off to sleep with visions of "sugarplums" falling from the heavens! As my dreams progressed, I experienced many different tastes coming down to me: chocolate cake, caramel topping, raspberry sauce, hot fudge, and so on. (Obviously, I did not have anything sweet at my evening meal before retiring.) Who would have thought that the Big Dipper was so full of calories? In fact, judging from the waistline of my pants I was sure I weighed more the following morning! Can you believe you can actually gain weight during your sleep by merely dreaming about fattening foods? Life is just too unfair for those who struggle hourly with weight issues.

At any rate, it was quite a celestial performance as I lay in bed and slowly drifted off to sleep within my rooftop aerie. There were so many wonders within this view, not to mention the differing rooflines and chimneys I looked out upon. Probably as many different people in the houses, or birds in the trees, as there were stars in the sky. At any rate, it was not difficult to fall asleep with so many comforting signs of nature surrounding oneself. It also gave the perspective of how small and insignificant we are in comparison with the universe. It must be much like God's eye view toward each of us. We are just a portion of our surroundings, one piece of the puzzle, one element of His concern. For this, I am grateful to be included.

The Art that Touched Me

It was a warm spring day and I decided to take a look at the shops on the other side of High Street. In the midst of the yellow and gray stone of the Cotswold buildings, this flash of color splashed on me just as a ray of sunshine bursts through the clouds. The overhead sign said Le Bel Artist Fine Art Studio. In the window was a large painting that had lines like Picasso, but colors like Andy Warhol. The pigments were so delightful that they lured me inside. It was there that I met Davis, the Managing Director of Le Bel, and he told me about the artwork they were featuring. The lovely colors, symmetry, and lines were stress-free, and the composition was very balanced. Davis explained that the artist was originally from Cambodia, which gave him much inspiration. How could this be? Had the artist not lived in Cambodia during all the strife? I had been a demonstrator during the Vietnam War, and my visions of the area were much different.

After viewing all the artwork and sadly realizing I could not afford any of this remarkable work, Davis invited me back later in the week for some "bubbly" and a visit with Ran, the artist. He now lives in the UK after studying in several different countries. I felt so honored to meet this gentle man, whose art spoke to me.

Ran told me about each painting and some of the history of his country. When I asked him where all the beautiful colors came from, he told me, "We have choices. I choose to be happy and paint happy." He shared with me some of his artistic influences and the many countries that have copies of his work. In the past, he often just gave a painting away to people who loved his work. Could I dare to hope?

Ran showed me his "magic stick" that he used to sketch initially. He did not use a brush, but a piece of whittled wood that he stroked with the flat edge in black paint to make the initial outline of his subject(s). He produced the same stick he had always used and the fact that he let me hold it was taking a great risk on his part. We had many varying discussions about each painting. He'd ask me what I saw in them, and he would tell me his interpretation of each piece; then we would laugh at what the other saw and find the similarities. It was such a precious hour, to be with a man of such history, passion, and talent and who would take the time to discuss his life and art with me. When we parted, he asked me to find his old friend and fellow artist, Louis, who resided in California. I was able to google him and find the gallery in Venice Beach where he had just completed an exhibit. I forwarded all the information on to Davis at Le Bel to give to Ran.

Over the years, I have visited many times with Ran and his beautiful wife. I have two of his paintings on my wall in San Diego, which remind me of the whimsical place in Cambodia and a most delightful artist who chooses to "paint happy."

"Creativity takes courage." ~ *Henri Matisse*

"A picture is a poem without words." ~ *Horace*

W
Wandering, Waiting, and Wellies

Wanderings

During my summers in the Cotswolds, I took several opportunities to see some of the sites in the English countryside, as well as a few European delights.

At least once a month during the summer, the North Cotswold National Trust Society organizes a trip via a motor coach to a destination Castle, Manor House, Cathedral, or Estate Gardens. I have enjoyed many of these trips throughout England and Wales.

I have also traveled with my British friend Dee to Guernsey (in the British Channel Islands), the Chelsea Flower Show, and Barcelona, Spain.

I have put on my big girl panties and made solo trips to Norway; Chartres, Giverny and Paris, France; Isle of Wight, and Iona, Scotland. All of these trips have been memorable and life-changing events—sailing the Fjords in Norway, walking the labyrinth in Chartres Cathedral, strolling through Monet's Garden in Giverny, and feeling the spirit and solitude of Iona. How lucky am I?

I am fortunate enough to have friends who enjoy traveling as much as I do. U.S. friends M and M have stayed with me in my village several times, as well as planned wonderful trips over the past summers. The beautiful places we have enjoyed together include Torquay, Dover, and Chester. Each trip was filled with laughter and good liquor and the revisiting of wonderful memories we have shared over the past fifty years. But our most spectacular trip yet was meeting in Amsterdam. What a wonderful city. One of our more memorable meals included dessert of a white powder, presented to us a round mirror with four straws. The server, no doubt used to the shocked expressions of the patrons, promptly instructed us to "suck it up, not snort it." The delightful powder was a mixture of white chocolate, coconut, and pop rocks. One never knows what to expect from the local humor in the way of "adventure."

"All journeys have secret destinations of which the traveler is unaware." ~ Martin Buber

Sharing Wonders in the USA

During my various summers in the UK, I have gotten to know Dee and her family. I have been fortunate to be chauffeured around the county by her and taking various trips together, including Guernsey and Barcelona. Her family have also given me rides to and from the airport, doctor appointments, and various lunch dates. I owe Dee a great deal in meeting many townspeople, wonderful excursions, and sharing much laughter.

Several summers, I booked Dee a flight home with me to see some of the wonders of the USA. One year, we stopped in Chicago to visit with my daughter and son-in-law and enjoy all that beautiful city has to offer. Another year we traveled to Sedona, Arizona and took the train from Williams to the Grand Canyon. We have stayed on Knob Hill, walked the labyrinth in Grace Cathedral, eaten on Fisherman's Wharf, and trekked through Alcatraz in San Francisco. We have taken the train from San Diego to Santa Barbara and enjoyed some of the Missions along the way. We have also cruised South out of San Diego to visited Cabo San Lucas, Mazatlan, and Puerto Villarta, in Baja Mexico.

Each and every trip has been exciting to see through Dee's eyes, and relive these several times over the years. How profoundly lucky we are to have discovered a lasting friendship and shared in multiple adventures over these past eight years. You just never know who you will meet that will change your life.

"I have found out that there ain't no surer way to find out whether you like people or hate them than to travel with them." ~ Mark Twain

Waiting...

On any journey, part of the adventure is waiting. This can be most difficult for some, but it can also accompany several of the best memories. In my little village, I take the bus everywhere. Because transportation is so accessible, I don't even entertain the notion of renting a car and driving. For on thing, there is the whole driving on the "wrong" side issue, as well as the steering wheel relocated to the right of the dashboard, the entering and leaving the multitude of roundabouts, and the narrow lanes and infrequent lay-bys to navigate.

Therefore, waiting at the bus stop is my way of life. I am frequently joined by the local pensioners, as they travel free on the bus system. It takes awhile to learn the bus jargon, such as a "single" versus "return" ticket, which side of the street the drop-offs and pick-ups are located, and where to sit on the bus—avoiding the handicapped seats, a long way forward of the school students, and as far from the drunks as possible. The bus drivers pride themselves on keeping to their schedule, so frequently the journey between stops resembles Mr. Toad's Wild Ride at Disneyland. That's why the wait at the bus stop is so important for relaxation in preparing for the jaunt ahead.

You also meet the most interesting people at the bus stop—visitors from out of town asking directions and sharing various sites they have seen; locals who know the best places to shop for sausages and leeks; and fellow Americans who want to hear all about living in the UK.

Equally as interesting is waiting for the train, whether in the station or on the platform. All kinds of people, from all different countries, with varying stories of travel to share. They especially like to talk with Americans about politics, places of interest, and Hollywood. My favorite remark was from a lovely Scotsman who confided in me about his relative living in the US. His query was, "I have a cousin living in Minnesota; do you know him?" You see, their maps of Great Britain and our USA are printed on the same size paper, thereby giving the illusion of them being the same size. There is no explanation that will change their minds as to the insignificance of the "colonies."

Lastly, waiting in the queue is a way of life and not to be dismissed lightly. It is a wonderful opportunity to meet the locals, share the gossip, or learn of the latest Brexit news and views of the current Prime Minister (which has changed three times during my summer sojournes). Comparing policy of Boris Johnson and Donald Trump is always good fodder for discussion.

"Life is not about waiting for the storm to pass. It's about learning to dance in the rain." ~ Unknown

New Wellies

I love to shop for shoes, in all cultures, in all countries, in all sorts of stores. But my most memorable spree was to purchase the famous waterporoof boots worn by British Aristocrats and farmers alike: the Wellington. This leather boot was first named for Arthur Wellesley, then first Duke of Wellington. Although the boot has undergone many changes since the early nineteenth century, it remains the most practical form of boot worn in all types of weather and for any occasion. I have seen women in wellies with their Sunday dresses, farmers mucking out manure in wellies handed down from their fathers, and children shod in multicolored boots for their trek to/from school.

The most popular wellies you see today are the olive drab polyurethane version that are molded to slip on and off with ease. However, this is somewhat of a misnomer, as it typically takes a partner or a good boot jack for assistance in removal.

Living in small UK villages, walking through the sheep fields, strolling in the rain, or mucking in the mud are all good reasons for owning a good pair of wellies. So off to the shoe shoppe I went to purchase my first pair. I knew it was popular to have the olive green or black versions, but I wanted to be different. I found a lovely pair of blue and white stripped boots adorned with a flashy red silk ribbon bow. These beauties will last a lifetime and be handed down to my daughter some day. (I know she is waiting with baited breath!) You know you have reached the "local" distinction in a village when you show up at the co-op in your wellies.

W - Wandering, Waiting, and Wellies | 179

"I'm too sexy for my boots..."

"On the farm, rubber boots go with anything. Especially pajamas." ~ unknown

X
X-Rays

There is nothing like a beautiful morning to pull you out of doors to stroll the High Street. One particular morning, I ventured in a different direction to peruse some of the establishments and gardens on the lower end of the village. I had just decided to get a cup of tea at one of my local breweries when I happened upon a raise in the sidewalk. Usually, I am very careful, as the sidewalks are the original ones poured just after the discovery of concrete and they have lost their original smoothness. Then down I went! Without a second thought, I was sitting on the ground wondering just how I was going to upright myself. There was a parked car within arm's length, but I had visions of pulling myself up on the bumper and setting off the alarm.

A lovely woman came running from across the street to assist, but she was about as big around as a sparrow. There was no way she would be able to lift my girth to a vertical position. I tried to roll over on all fours to get up, but my left wrist could not withstand any weight. I sat there for a few minutes assessing my situation, when a delightful young man came running and without thinking lifted me up from behind as though I was weightless. Not only was he young and strong, but exceptionally easy on the eyes. There is a God!

I tried to thank him, but he was off in a flash, probably afraid I would ask him to walk me home. The lady who had come to assist advised me to "take more water with my drink the next time." She obviously thought I had just emerged from the pub and had decided I might be a bit tipsy. For heaven's sake, it was only 10:30 in the morning!

I babied the wrist for the rest of the day, but made an appointment for an x-ray for the next morning. Our village is lucky enough to have a local surgery (aka doctor's office) and dentist, but no x-ray machine. So it meant a trip on the bus and a half-mile walk to the local hospital. The x-ray was inconclusive, as I have a lot of arthritis in my wrists. The nurse made me an appointment to see the orthopedist at the hospital in Cheltanham the next week. That hospital is about thirty-five miles away, so I had to organize a ride versus the bus and taxi.

I emerged from the A&E (that's a British ER) with a lovely white cast on my arm to sport around for the next six weeks. I will say it provided a lot of unnecessary attention, but I healed up quickly and as I look back on the event, it didn't stop me from enjoying any outings or good times. I felt very lucky to have received such a relatively small injury. As well, a special thanks to the handsome young man who helped me up that fateful day. The British are forever helpful.

X - X-Rays | 183

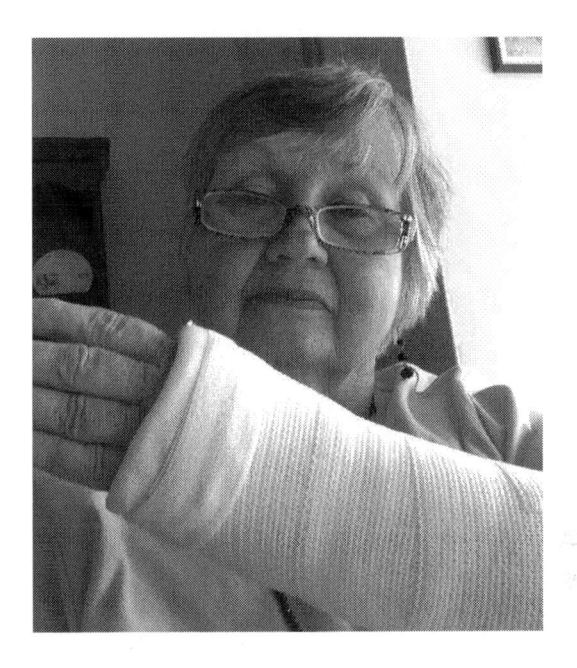

"Sometimes it takes a good fall to really know where you stand." ~ Hayley Williams

Y
The Year 2020

The year began much like the past eight years. I had secured my cottage for that summer before I left in September 2019. I had paid off my rent in increments and three months were assured for my one-bedroom flat that I had stayed in some years previous. In January 2020, I booked my flight for the end of May. I had also found a cruise I was interested in that would take me to all the areas that were on my European bucket list: the South of France, Lisbon, Dubrovnik, and Athens. Following that trip, I would get back into the States by mid September. The itinerary for the summer was beyond fantastic.

The first of February 2020, I came down with a type of flu that was the worst I had ever had. Although I was never hospitalized, I didn't totally recover from it for almost a month. I remember thinking how lucky I was to have gotten sick where medical care was easily accessible. And then in March, the world came to a stand-still. The coronavirus was officially diagnosed and COVID-19 began its spread throughout the world. At first, we all thought it would pass quickly; however, different areas of the globe treated the spread of the disease in varying degrees. I was still holding out hope of returning to my beloved village up until April 2020, when British Air cancelled all flights out of the US into England. How could this happen? I had planned so carefully. But people were dying of this disease and no cure in the site. The world was officially in a pandemic!

So much for my plans for the summer. Quarantine was the new normal. People who were lucky enough to have a job were working from home. Businesses, schools, churches, sporting events, restaurants—all closed. There were shortages of toilet paper, hand sanitizer, and disinfectant wipes. It felt like a bad sci-fi movie. People were wearing masks everywhere and encouraged to social distance if they had to leave the house. And I was officially hosting my own pity party on a daily basis.

How long would this crisis last? It was still unknown. Though more and more people are being vaccinated each day, the pandemic, and periodic lockdowns, have continued into 2021.

Despite the disappointment of no travel during 2020, I used my summer creatively. I completed the musings I had been accumulating from previous summers and put them in book form. I have booked my flight to London for June 2021 and remain hopeful I will be able to make the trip. This also means I will have to come up with another excuse ("I'm researching a book") to give to the Customs agents at Heathrow. Of course, there could always be a sequel to write.

"I told my suitcases that there will be no vacation this year. Now I'm dealing with emotional baggage."
~ unknown

Z
Zenith

'Zenith': (noun) The time at which something is most powerful or successful; culminating point. Have I reached it? Most definitely *not*, as I am not dead yet! I plan to continue my summers in the UK for as long as this feeble body can still move, and I am able to sit up and take nourishment. And when the day comes that my doctor advises me to no longer travel, or my children worry over my "state of mind," or my money runs out, then and only then will I give up this lifestyle. I am just shy of my ten year goal, due to the pandemic, but hope I am not limited from carrying on even longer.

There have been a few changes in my little village in that many shops on the High Street have closed or opened under different management. We say goodbye to old friends and welcome new ones. Among the most significant loss of friends has been my dear friend Barry, who instilled such a love of the Cotswolds in me. The village has also lost other significant locals, including Lady Kings Norton, Jecca, Dr. Jennifer, Audrey, and Mr. Cooper. Other dear ones from our Methodist Church have also left us, including Nora, Brian, Colin, Mary, and Pauline. I still feel their presence whenever I am there and am so grateful to have had them in my life.

In my California home, there is a bit of the Cotswolds in every room. Not everyone would notice them, but I see the subtle artifacts every day. I also keep my family pictures, the Stars and Stripes, and a favorite tea cup stored at Dee's house in the UK. They await my return, as well as all my British friends.

"Zenith" merely refers to the end of this book of musings. The gift of my dual status between the two countries will hopefully continue for a few more years. Thank you for sharing some of my wonderful memories and I hope it encourages you to break out of your "safe place" and create adventures of your own.

"Memory marks the horizon of our consciousness, imagination its zenith." ~ Amos Bronson Alcott

"I find my zenith doth depend upon a most auspicious star, who's influcence if now I court not, but omit, my fortunes will ever after droop." ~ William Shakespeare

ABOUT MARILYN HONEA

Marilyn Honea is a writer, former Speech/Language Pathologist, volunteer, and avid traveler. Following retirement and the loss of her husband, Marilyn began reevaluating her life and eventually set upon a new adventure in the English countryside. Since then, she has spent four to six months each year with the delightful residents of a small village in the Cotswolds. When not sharing "a cuppa" with them on a rainy day, Marilyn lives in Southern California, where she spends time with her grown children and friends.

ACKNOWLEDGMENTS

Even though this year of 2020 has had its challenges, I am so very grateful for the time to put words to paper and share my adventures with you, the reader. I was blessed to share some time in the Cotswolds with friends from the U.S., including Danielle, my Mum Mary, Mark & Mary, Pennie, Torrey, Jerrie and Ralph, Clarice and Gary, Carol, Steve & Karen, Neena, Barb and Dan, Cathy, Beth and Katie, and Ruthe. Our time together was priceless and I am thankful to have you in my life.

I couldn't make this yearly trek without the support of my family in the USA. I love and cherish you and am grateful for you keeping the home fires burning.

As well, I would like to thank the talented people at Powerful You! Publishing for making this labor of love possible. Sue Urda, your words of encouragement have carried me through a most enjoyable process. Dana Micheli, your editing skills have lightened my load and made writing almost stress-free. Thank you as well to Kathy Fyler for your assistance with graphics and photographs. I am indebted to all of you for your creative skills and enjoying my sense of humor.

"You can't go back and change the beginning, but you can start where you are and change the ending."
~ C.S. Lewis

Made in the USA
Coppell, TX
26 June 2021